Art and Nonart

Art and Nonart

Reflections on an Orange Crate
and a Moose Call

Marcia Muelder Eaton

Rutherford ● Madison ● Teaneck
Fairleigh Dickinson University Press
London and Toronto: Associated University Presses

Associated University Presses, Inc.
4 Cornwall Drive
East Brunswick, NJ 08816

Associated University Presses Ltd
27 Chancery Lane
London WC2A 1NF, England

Associated University Presses
2133 Royal Windsor Drive
Unit 1
Mississauga, Ontario, L5J 1K5, Canada

Library of Congress Cataloging in Publication Data

Eaton, Marcia Muelder, 1938–
  Art and nonart.

  Bibliography: p.
  Includes index.
  1. Art—Philosophy. I. Title.
N71.E2 1983   701   81-65462
ISBN 0-8386-3084-7

Printed in the United States of America

For Joe

Contents

Acknowledgements

I wish to thank the following for having given me permission to quote from published works:

Almqvist & Wiksell Förlag AB and Teddy Brunius for permission to quote from Teddy Brunius, *Theory and Taste*, 1969.

Basil Blackwell Publisher and The University of California Press for permission to quote from *Ludwig Wittgenstein, Lectures and Conversations on Aesthetics, Psychology, and Religious Belief*, 1972.

The Bodley Head, Ltd., and Alfred A. Knopf, Inc. for permission to quote from Ford Madox Ford, *The Good Soldier*, 1951.

Cambridge University Press for permission to quote from Walter Hooper, editor, *Selected Literary Essays*, 1969.

Chatto & Windus Ltd and Mrs. Q. D. Leavis and New York University Press for permission to quote from F. R. Leavis, *The Great Tradition*, 1973.

Clarendon Press for permission to quote from Bernhard Berenson, *The Italian Painters of the Renaissance*, 1930.

Cornell University Press for permission to quote from George Dickie, *Art and Aesthetics*, 1974.

Hafner Press and Macmillan Publishing Co. for permission to quote from Immanuel Kant, *Critique of Judgment*, 1963.

The Hamlyn Publishing Group, Ltd. for permission to quote from Bernard Myers and Trevin Coppleston, editors, *Art Treasures in Spain*, 1969.

Harcourt Brace Jovanovich, Inc. for permission to quote from Jack Hobbs, *Art in Context*, 1975.

Harcourt Brace Jovanovich, Inc. for permission to quote from René Wellek and Austin Warren, *Theory of Literature*, 1956.

William Heinemann Ltd. and Loganesi e C for permission to quote from Guido Ballo, *The Critical Eye*, 1969.

Hogarth Press and Mrs. Katherine Jones for permission to quote from Ernest Jones, *Essays in Applied Psychoanalysis*, 1964.

I wish to thank the following for use of visual materials:

Walker Art Center, Minneapolis, Minnesota for permission to reproduce Mark di Suvero, *Stuyyesants Eye*.

Musée Marmottan and S. A. Studio Lournmel 77 for permission to reproduce Claude Monet, *Impression: Sunrise*.

National Gallery of Art, Washington, D.C. for permission to reproduce Rembrandt Van Ryn, *The Descent from the Cross*.

The Louvre and Cliché Musées Nationaux, Paris, for permission to reproduce Theodore Géricault, *The Raft of the Medusa*.

Carl-Erick Ström and Tryckerigruppen, Malmö, Sweden, for permission to reproduce Carl-Erick Ström, *Man Looking Out to Sea*.

Metropolitan Museum of Art, New York, for permission to reproduce El Greco, *View of Toledo*.

The Art Institute of Chicago for permission to reproduce Paul Cézanne, *The Plate of Apples*.

Kunstmuseum, Lucerne, for permission to reproduce Bjørn Nørgard, *Pig Heads on Pedestals*.

Fogg Art Museum, Harvard University, Cambridge, Massachusetts for permission to reproduce Honoré Daumier, *European Equilibrium*.

Jack Ohman for permission to reproduce *There, It's Balanced*.

Albright-Knox Art Gallery, Buffalo, New York for permission to reproduce Arshile Gorky, *The Liver is the Cock's Comb*.

©Arch. Phot., Paris/ SPADEM/ VAGA, New York for permission to reproduce a photograph of the Arc de Triomphe d'Etoile.

Connecticut Department of Economic Development for permission to reproduce a photograph of Carl Andre, *Stone Field*.

Thorvaldsen's Museum, Copenhagen for permission to reproduce Berthel Thorvaldsen, *Christ*.

The Coca-Cola Company for permission to reproduce a photograph of an Early Coke Bottle.

The University of Minnesota Photo Lab for their help in preparing and permission to reproduce a photograph of a souvenir wallhanging and of Lee's *Seated Girl*.

Rijksmuseum, Amsterdam for permission to reproduce Jan Vermeer, *Maidservant Pouring Milk*.

The Old Corner House, Stockbridge, Massachusetts, for permission to reproduce Norman Rockwell, *The Marriage License*.

Musei Vaticani, Rome, for permission to reproduce Michelangelo, *The Prophet Isaiah*.

The Saturday Evening Post and The Curtis Publishing Company for permission to reproduce Norman Rockwell, *Rosie the Riveter*.

Trustees of the Wallace Collection, London for permission to reproduce Sir Joshua Reynolds, *Strawberry Girl*.

Minneapolis Tribune for permission to reproduce a cartoon by Richard · Guindon.

I am also indebted to several people for help in writing this book. My colleagues at the University of Minnesota, particularly Allen Buchanan, Richard Leppert, Homer and Joan Mason, Michael and Tamara Root, Sandra Peterson, Rolf Sartorius, and John Wallace, were especially helpful. I am grateful to the Philosophy Institute and Royal Library in Copenhagen for providing research facilities, and to the Danish National Bank for supporting my research during the 1977–78 academic year. I wish also to thank Peter Kivy of Rutgers University for his many insightful and helpful suggestions. My research assistant, Jacqueline Henkel, provided invaluable criticism and help with editing and manuscript preparation, as did my secretary, Meredith Poppele.

Finally, I must acknowledge my husband, Joe, and son, Dennis. Without them, this book might have been finished sooner, but certainly would have meant less.

Art and Nonart

1

Reflections on an Orange Crate and a Moose Call

i. Introduction

There is a great deal of skepticism in aesthetics with respect to the possibility of finding a definition for the term 'work of art'. Morris Weitz, for one, contends that, by its very nature, the concept defies definition. He believes that the necessary and sufficient conditions for an object's being a work of art cannot be stated. Using Wittgenstein's notion of a family resemblance, Weitz likens 'art' to 'game' and insists that at best the activities falling under them resemble only some of the other members of the family. Both 'art' and 'game' are "open concepts" according to Weitz: the conditions under which they apply are constantly changing; when we use these terms we remain always open to correction and emendation. In contrast, mathematical and logical concepts, concepts whose necessary and sufficient conditions can be stated, are "closed," and their use is strictly limited. But open concepts remain flexible in the sense that we can always imagine situations in which applying them calls for a decision or interpretation on our part.[1]

Certainly we are aware of the difficulties we encounter in attempting to define even such commonplace, everyday concepts as 'chair' or 'animal'. Borderline cases, such as oversized beanbags and viruses, can cause problems. And there are additional difficulties for defining 'work of art'. As Weitz says, "The very expansive, adventurous character of art, its ever-present changes and novel creations, make it logically impossible to ensure any set of defining properties."[2] The creative aspects of artistic activity necessitate that the concept 'work of art' be always open. If, for example, 'is a painting' were definable, then limits would be placed on what painters could do. But creativity itself demands that no limitations be placed on what painters can do;

15

therefore 'is a painting' cannot be defined. The case is alleged to be the same for all other art forms. Furthermore, the term 'art' is used both descriptively (to identify the class to which an object belongs) and normatively (to evaluate an object). Weitz believes that there is no set of defining properties that can capture both functions of the term.

One obvious conclusion to draw from this line of argument is that there is no way of determining whether or not something is a work of art. Many people are untroubled by this position, believing that, after all, art is everywhere and everything; like beauty, it is simply in the eye of the beholder. In part, this attitude springs from our constantly being reminded that great artists in the past were not accepted or appreciated in their own time. Popular biographies of individuals such as Van Gogh or Gauguin stress the suffering inflicted upon them by a public unable to see what even the least sophisticated of us is able to see today. We are implicitly and explicitly warned not to be the fools our predecessors were, that it is essential to keep an open mind. Hilton Kramer emphasizes the effect all this has had on what we are now willing to call a 'work of art'.

> We are ready, if not always willing or happy, to accept as a work of art almost any object, arrangement of objects or sheer physical gesture that someone identifying himself as an artist asserts to be a work of art. Almost? I am not even sure this "almost" any longer obtains. The guilt of the past acts as a brake on spontaneous tendencies to skepticism.[3]

We thus find a widespread tolerance to accept as 'art' whatever artists say it is, or, as I find among many students, a readiness to believe that art is whatever moves you.

Others, myself included, are unwilling to believe that everything and anything is a work of art. In spite of the elusiveness of a set of defining properties, the move to a purely subjective position is unattractive at best. It is my intention here to present a theory which will provide a way of dealing with this skepticism with respect to distinguishing art from nonart.

Weitz likens 'art' to 'game'; so let us consider the latter term briefly to see if the properties they share really support his skeptical position. We must agree with Wittgenstein that it is certainly difficult to say what it is that basketball, squash, chess, bridge, pick-up-sticks, and patience have in common. First attempts to identify necessary or sufficient conditions for these games, definitions involving properties such as 'competitiveness' and 'amusement', are quickly thwarted. I have played games of bridge when it was quite clear that no one was being amused. And even if the notion of competition against oneself or a deck of cards (as in patience) could be made sense of, competition is certainly not a sufficient condition; a great many competitive activities are certainly not games.

Throughout our childhood, my younger brother engaged in an activity which the family called "throwing the ball against the wall." It consisted simply of my brother's throwing a small rubber ball against the outside of our house and then catching, or trying to catch it (with imitations of cheering crowds when appropriate). Clearly, he was playing; but was he playing a 'game'? What would one have to know in order to answer this question? And suppose we find an answer? What have we gained? Can we now *do* or *say* anything we couldn't do or say before?

Such questions lie behind both Wittgenstein's and Weitz's positions. Each believes that the proper business of philosophy (and hence of aesthetics) lies in attacking other problems. But their positions on the indefinability of certain terms can be very misleading if one concludes, for example, "Well then, everything must be a game," or "Everything must or can, then, be a work of art." Wittgenstein or Weitz did not, it must be emphasized, come to either of these conclusions. But their work can be used as support by people sympathetic to the "Everything is art" point of view.

Now we might benefit from looking at 'game' from an angle neither Wittgenstein nor Weitz considered. Suppose we are standing in an observation balcony overlooking an operating room where a team of surgeons is performing open-heart surgery. One of the observers says, "This is the best game of the season." Surely, the observer has made a mistake in referring to what is going on below as a 'game'.[4] The surgeons are certainly not playing one. Why? The answer to this question will tell us a great deal about the concept.

Even Weitz believes that aesthetics properly engaged in will attempt "to give a logical description of the actual functioning of the concept, including a description of the conditions under which we use it ['work of art'] or its correlates."[5] He failed, however, to recognize the value of the strategy of looking at incorrect uses of such terms. A fairly simple word like 'chair' is difficult to define if one looks only at examples of what we all agree to be chairs—rockers, straightbacks, overstuffed chairs, and beanbags. But when we ask, "Why aren't stools chairs?" we see that at least a necessary condition for something's being a chair is that it provide back support. Of course, this might occur to someone who considers only the class of objects that we all agree are chairs. But I am claiming that a useful tactic is to consider things that are not members of the class. Thus part of the strategy of this work shall be to look at some incorrect uses of 'work of art', as well as paradigm uses.

One reason, I think, that we encounter so many people who are ready to say that everything is art is that art in the twentieth century has developed as it

Fig. 1. Mark di Suvero, *Stuyvesants Eye*. Walker Art Center, Minneapolis, Minnesota, gift of the T. B. Walker Foundation.

has. People fry eggs, cut up horses, and dig holes, all *in* the name of art and *with* the name 'art.' This is not to say that all art in the twentieth century consists of "borderline cases." The onslaught of oversized bean bags did not suddenly produce a radical change in the concept 'chair'. Yet our concepts do change, and the nature of artistic activity probably changes our notions about works of art more rapidly. There are, in our contemporary culture, more borderline works of art—cases which we find puzzling—than borderline chairs, and this has caused fairly widespread (but, as I hope to show, unwarranted) despair. (See figure 1.)

Although this proliferation of borderline cases may account in part for the readiness to say, "Everything's a work of art," it must be pointed out that confusion about whether or not an object counts as an artwork is not limited to cases involving only things created in our century. A crude third-century headdress or ornately carved eighteenth-century commode may just as readily lead one to ask, "Is that art?" Consequently the theory of art I propose is not intended to deal exclusively with problems of modern art, or to explain the special nature of modernism. Even though the twentieth century has crystallized them in the minds of a growing segment of the population, the philosophical problems we confront in this discussion have been with us much longer.

A second reason why people sometimes think the term 'work of art' refers to everything is that they often confuse 'work of art' and 'aesthetic object', and in this book I shall try to show that the two are different. All of the skillets in the world can be looked at aesthetically, but not all of them are works of art; some bridges may be works of art—but not all are, though all are potentially aesthetic objects. The basis of this distinction will become clearer later. For now, suffice it to say that if everything is a work of art, then saying that something is a work of art should have no more effect than saying, "It's a thing" has. And this is clearly not the case.

There is one more point we must make before turning to the main discussion. It could be objected, with good reason, I think, that it makes absolutely no difference whether or not we decide to call my brother's play a 'game'. The nature and value of his activity remains the same regardless of how we name it. If this discussion is to be worthwhile, then I shall have to convince the reader, not only that we can determine whether or not something should be called a work of art, but that that decision is of some consequence.

ii. The Puzzle

Developments in modern art have time and again forced us to consider the following kind of case. Imagine six people and a philosopher strolling together through a sculpture garden filled with classical and contemporary pieces. A hedge-lined path suddenly opens into a small section of meticulously clipped lawn. In the middle of the grass is an empty orange crate in front of which is a plaque that reads "Number 31." While the group stands looking at it, a gardener comes along, puts down another orange crate identical to the first, and proceeds to look for and pull up crabgrass.

The philosopher smiles and suggests that the original crate be called "A," the newly placed crate "B," and asks for comments. We can imagine members of the group responding in the following way.

Adams: "A is an artwork, but B isn't."
Bates: "Neither A nor B is an artwork."
Carlson: "A and B make up a new artwork, C."
Davis: "A is an artwork and B is an artwork."
Evans: "If A is an artwork, then B is an artwork."
Franklin: "A *was* an artwork, but the gardener ruined it."

What, if anything, can the philosopher do to arbitrate? Mere insistence that the individuals justify their claims only intensifies the disagreement. It is claimed on the one hand by Adams that the exact placement of the crate matters essentially and hence that only A qualifies. On the other hand, Davis maintains that all that can matter aesthetically are the intrinsic properties of an object, and hence, both A and B are artworks. Bates responds that this is precisely why neither is. Franklin, who doesn't know much about art, but who does know what he likes, feels that the gardener has interfered in what used to be an artistic situation. Evans, who knows a lot about art but who doesn't know what he likes, prefers material implication. What began as a pleasant afternoon threatens to degenerate quickly into petulance and hostility.

In desperation, the philosopher suggests that the issues might be made clearer if a slightly different but analogous case is considered. The group is asked to imagine attending a musical revue at which one of the acts is this. A large moose, stage-named "B," lumbers out onto the stage followed by a medium-sized person, stage-named "A." A opens her mouth and produces a loud call. B does the same, in fact utters a sound indistinguishable from that of A. Notice how easy it is to revise the above comments in such a way that they still apply.

Adams: "A is an artist, B is not."
Bates: "Neither A nor B is an artist."
Carlson: "A and B make up a team of artists."
Davis: "A is an artist and B is an artist."
Evans: "If A is an artist, then B is an artist."
Franklin: "A might be an artist, but not with that moose on stage."

Or,

Adams: "The noise made by A is an art work, but the noise made by B is not."
Bates: "Neither noise made is an art work."
Carlson: "The noises together make up a new art work."
Davis: "Both noises are art works."
Evans: "If the noise made by A is an art work, then so is the noise made by B."
Franklin: "The noise made by A would be an art work if not made so close to B."

In support of their claims, Bates, Carlson, Davis, and Evans make references to intrinsic properties. They ask the others to consider what would happen if the persons were taken into the theater blindfolded. The result here would be that no aesthetic distinction could possibly be made between A and B. When it is *sounds* we are concerned with, surely the accidental fact that we can see a moose or a woman can't matter. Similarly, it is the orange crate as a visual object we are assessing or describing; we are not concerned with who put it down. Yet Adams and Franklin assert that the fact that intrinsic properties alone do not allow for discrimination between A and B proves that these properties alone are not all that count.

Lest the reader think that these examples are too farfetched to bear consideration, allow me to call attention to three different real-life situations in which we are likely to fall into the same sort of puzzlement.

1. "It won't be long," the copying-machine salesman told me, "before we can make copies indistinguishable from the original. We'll even be able to reproduce the piles of pigment on that painting on your wall." Will I be able then to return my painting to the University Gallery with no sense of loss?

2. At Lascaux they are building a simulated cave for visitors—a cave indistinguishable from the original—in order to protect the real site from the wear of traffic. Should visitors care which cave they are in?

3. A pass receiver fumbles a pass to another pass receiver from the same team who happens to be standing behind him. As the second pass receiver runs by the first he fumbles the ball back into his hands. The whole process is repeated and a touchdown is scored. "I just love slop like that," says one announcer. But the other announcer points out that the team has been practicing that play all week. Not only must our description be modified ("fumble" is no longer an appropriate label), but a different kind of delight is appropriate.

As I have already suggested, a fundamental disagreement at the core of these kinds of disputes is waged in connection with the so-called intrinsic properties of objects. One side of the debate is exemplified by this remark made by Mario de Micheli:

Like all other impressionists, Cézanne inherited from Courbet a hatred for fantasy and the literary element in art. A painting, in his view, must live by the strength of the paint alone, must rely only on the means which are proper to it, without the aid of melodrama or anecdote.[6]

Some persons, like Davis in the sculpture garden example above, insist that the only thing that can matter aesthetically is an object in itself. The only properties that count are those than can be *perceived directly*, that is, those properties that do not depend upon knowledge deriving from sources outside of the object itself. It is the way something sounds, not the cause of the sound, that counts; and it is the way an object looks, not who made it look that way or why anyone wanted it to look that way, that is important in aesthetic consideration of the object. Formal properties—color, sound, meter, shape, pitch—are obviously one kind of intrinsic property, and many theorists would have us consider only them. Others grant that some nonformal properties such as subject matter may also be relevant, but only as long as the viewer or hearer can perceive these within the work itself.

The other side of the debate is represented fictionally above in the comments of Adams and Franklin. That is, one might turn to properties not intrinsic to the artistic object itself in order to develop a definition for 'work of art'. Considerations that might be included under the heading "extrinsic properties" will become more apparent in the next chapter when we consider references to them in detail. Many descriptions of works of art point to facts about them that, unlike colors, shapes, and size, cannot be seen just by observing them. Teddy Brunius, for instance, in discussing ways in which our perceptions of paintings can be altered by the particular descriptions given of them, points out that Monet originally entitled *Impression: Sunrise, The Harbor of Le Havre,* and claims that the title change "created, by means of the reactions of the critics, the name of the new way of painting, 'impressionism'."[7] That the painting underwent such a crucial title change cannot be discovered merely by looking at it, no matter how closely or carefully the looking is done. (See figure 2.)

I shall examine one position which argues for the supremacy of intrinsic properties of works of art, viz., the anti-intentionalist position, in chapter 2, section iv. But a brief description of the general stand is in order here. There seem to be two sorts of reasons that lead people to believe that in aesthetic contexts only reference to the intrinsic properties of objects matter. First, there are serious problems which arise in all theories or views which allow for or insist upon reference to extrinsic properties. Second, in discussions of works of art we must attend to the work, and information which concerns something that cannot be perceived is distracting. Reference to what cannot

Fig. 2. Claude Monet, *Impression: Sunrise.* **Musée Marmottan, S.A. Studio Lourmel 77, Photo Routhier.**

be perceived in the object will take us away from what we should be attending to.

The first sort of reason is compelling only if one examines all theories which allow reference to extrinsic properties, finds them wanting, and then proceeds to prove that all such theories *must* be found wanting. That there are serious problems for many such theories cannot be denied. Indeed, in chapter 2 I shall discuss several. The claim that all such theories must be found inadequate requires a general argument and usually relies for support on the second sort of reason, namely that reference to extrinsic properties distracts one from that to which one should be paying attention.

Such a position is taken by a wide variety of aestheticians. Edward Bullough, for example, believes that as viewers we must distance ourselves psychologically so as to put ourselves "out of gear with our practical self."[8] It is only by putting aside our normal interests and considerations that we are in a position to have a truly aesthetic experience. We can then look at an object "'objectively' . . . by permitting only such reactions on our part as emphasize the 'objective' features of the experience, and by interpreting even our 'subjective' affections not as modes of *our* being but rather as characteristics of the phenomenon."[9]

Similarly José Ortega y Gasset maintains that aesthetic or artistic experience and activity is marked by a removal of all practical or ordinary emotional involvement. He gives as an example a dying man whose bedside is attended by his wife, a doctor, a newspaper reporter, and a painter. The first three are involved emotionally and practically in differing degrees. But the painter, according to Ortega, is psychologically distanced from the event he represents. The artist,

> indifferent, merely glances sidewise at the human reality. What happens there does not worry him; he is, as they say, miles away from the event. His attitude is purely contemplative and one might even say that he does not contemplate the event in its integrity; the painful internal sense of it is left outside the field of his perception. He pays attention only to externals, to lights and shadows, to chromatic values. With the painter we have reached a point of maximum distance and of minimum sentimental intervention.[10]

The insistence that we put aside ordinary interests is also at the core of formalist theories such as those held by Roger Fry and Clive Bell. Consideration of content, according to these theorists, is an unaesthetic as worrying about how to make a dying man's last moments as comfortable as possible. Thus Fry says,

> Now I venture to say that no one who has a real understanding of the art of painting attaches any importance to what we call the subject of a picture— what is represented. To one who feels the language of pictorial form all depends upon *how* it is presented, nothing on what. Rembrandt expressed his profoundest feelings just as well when he painted a carcass hanging up in a butcher's shop as when he painted the Crucifixion or his mistress. Cézanne who most of us believe to be the greatest artist of modern times expressed some of his grandest conceptions in pictures of fruit and crockery on a common kitchen table.[11]

The best criticism of the so-called aesthetic attitude theories comes from George Dickie, in an article entitled "The Myth of the Aesthetic Attitude." There Dickie argues that we do not assume a special attitude when we look at certain things. Nor do we look at things in a special way. Rather we look at

Fig. 3. Rembrandt Van Ryn, *The Descent from the Cross*. National Gallery of Art, Washington, D.C., Widener Collection.

special things. The trouble with the wife of the dying man is not that she has the wrong attitude. It is that she is not paying attention to the right things.[12]

The greatest problem with "form over content" people is that it is difficult to understand exactly what we are supposed to do. If we grant that a painting does not derive its value from its subject matter, does it follow that we are not to pay any attention to the subject matter? When I look at a Rembrandt Crucifixion am I not supposed to notice that it is a Crucifixion? (See figure 3.) Can we see the form of a work without seeing the content—the way we look at a figure and see the duck without seeing the rabbit? (See figure 4.) Here too I think Dickie's line of criticism is appropriate. It is not that something wrong, something non-aesthetic, has been done when we notice that we have a painting of the body of Christ and not of a deer. Rather, it is that we must pay attention to other things as well.

Fig. 4. Ruth Anne Ruud, *Duck-Rabbit*. Courtesy of the artist.

But superior as Dickie's position is, I believe, to others, it still involves paying attention to some things rather than others. How do we know which things are the things we pay attention to when our experience is correctly to be called 'aesthetic'? Dickie does not specify what the things are that must be paid attention to if our contemplation is truly aesthetic. He certainly does not prove (or try to) that only intrinsic properties are candidates for the things to be paid attention to, and that no other properties are.

Fry does want to limit our attention to intrinsic properties. But he gives no convincing or even very persuasive reason for this:

In a loan exhibition I came upon a picture of Chardin. It was a signboard painted to hang outside a druggist's shop. It represented a number of glass retorts, a still, and various glass bottles, the furniture of a chemist's laboratory at that time. . . . Well, it gave me a very intense and vivid sensation. Just the shapes of those bottles and their mutual relations gave me the feeling of something immensely grand and impressive and the phrase that came into mind was, "This is just how I felt when I first saw Michelangelo's frescoes in the Sistine Chapel." Those represented the whole history of creation with the tremendous images of Sybils [*sic*] and Prophets, but esthetically it meant something very similar to Chardin's glass bottles.[13]

Are we to infer that thinking about creation is not important when looking at the Sistine Chapel frescoes? Is it in fact illegitimate? Fry is evidently able to recognize when he is having a "pure" aesthetic experience, and, at least in the example given, it has something (or everything) to do with shapes and their relationships to one another. A great deal more is needed if we are to share his understanding and recognize what we are to attend to, and if we are to be convinced that only those things are "aesthetic."

Psychical distance theorists are extremely fond of examples from nature. Edmund Burke, one of the first philosophers to make significant use of the concept of "disinterestedness" in aesthetics, used a storm at sea as his example. When we are at some distance from the sea storm, he says, when we are certain of our own safety, then we are free to take pleasure in it, to contemplate it as an aesthetic object.[14] This is a good example, for all of us have taken pleasure from watching waves beat against a shore, and, when seasick, have taken great displeasure in the same sort of sight. But as I stand securely and comfortably on shore, knowing that there is no danger of a tidal wave or seasickness, and as I enjoy the spectacle of the sea storm, how exactly am I to know whether my enjoyment is purely aesthetic? Fry, it seems, would have us overlook the fact that it is a sea or a storm that we are watching. This seems utter nonsense to me. Has something gone awry if we consider the physics involved or the capacity the water has for generating energy? Am I, or am I not, allowed to imagine what it might be like to be on an air mattress (not just a brightly colored rectangle) tossed about on those waves?

The enjoyment we have in the contemplation of something is extremely complex. Indentifying just the part of that enjoyment which is purely aesthetic is difficult, if possible at all. If the supremacy of intrinsic properties depends upon such an identification, then it rests on unfirm ground. For now, then, we shall remain open to the possibility that one may benefit from reference to extrinsic properties in discussions of works of art.

Thus far my examples have been mainly from the visual arts. Throughout the remainder of this book most of the examples will be taken from writings on literature and painting. The theory I shall propose, however, is not restricted to these art forms. The emphasis on literature and painting is due to the fact of my own greater familiarity with critical writings in these areas. As we turn to an examination of various ways in which people talk about art, referring as they do both to intrinsic and extrinsic properties, we shall consider instances of both visual and nonvisual arts. I have also attempted to cite a wide variety of sources in which we find discussions of works of art: newspapers as well as professional journals, program notes as well as historical volumes.

2
Talking about Works of Art

i. Introduction: The Function of Criticism

In order to define exactly what "works of art" are, I think we need to start, as
certainly others have, by examining not simply the objects that have been
separated off as "works of art," but also the larger context in which these
objects appear. In particular, I think a great deal can be learned from looking
at the way in which art objects are customarily treated. They are, at least
often, revered. They are scrutinized. And they are, at least often, held to be
the centers of valuable experiences. But, most important, they are *discussed*,
and these discussions reflect the basic assumptions we make about the nature
of art. The talking and writing that surrounds works of art is certainly one very
important part of their context, and of what has recently come to be called the
"institution of art."

The so-called institutional theories of art stress the importance of considering a work of art as part of a larger network of things. To understand this
larger network is, indeed, an important goal of aesthetics. The apparent
impossibility of defining 'art'—Weitz's arguments on this point have been very
influential—has led many theorists to redirect their attention in this fashion,
to give up a search for a property common to all works of art in favor of an
attempt to elucidate the multifarious factors that affect artistic activity. Teddy
Brunius, for instance, insists not only that we cannot "look at the arts as
members of a definite system," but that it is similarly a mistake to try to
produce a "theory of aesthetics."[1] He calls such theories "ideologies of taste"
and suggests that rather than concentrating on the traditional questions of
modern aesthetics we would do better to engage in "empirical aesthetics": the
examination of ways in which various cultures have dealt with individual
works and the ways in which these works intersect with prevailing cultural
norms. We can successfully, Brunius thinks, investigate the various "rules"

29

which different people in different places and times have used to determine which things are works of art and how they are to be used. "Like a horse in a game of chess, a work of art is also *a vehicle of rules*," he says. "When we agree that something is a work of art, we use it according to certain rules."[2] Each culture has its own, and these sets of rules are the proper object of study, not a mythical property that all aesthetic objects, activities, and experiences have in common.

Like Brunius, Søren Kjørup (and others, as we shall see later in this chapter) believes that the proper object of aesthetic investigation is the cultural context in which art works are created, although he is somewhat less skeptical than Brunius that a comprehensive theory of art or aesthetics can be developed. According to Kjørup, "You have to understand the Institution of Art as a whole before you can grasp what creating or proclaiming a work of art is, let alone what a work of art is as such."[3] He believes that the "Institution of Art" can be described, though admittedly with difficulty.

Although there are weaknesses with institutional theories of art (we shall look at them more closely later), I agree with Brunius and Kjørup that an understanding of art demands a consideration of more than individual objects. Playing around with words or colors or simply reacting positively or negatively to the shapes or sounds of an aesthetic object is essentially an individual experience. But the institutional or social nature of art comes about when ways and means are developed for sharing these experiences; and such sharing depends upon our being able to talk to one another about them. I believe that the *most* important part of the institution of art is located in the talking and writing that surrounds these art works.

In this chapter we shall, therefore, look at various ways in which people talk about art objects, always with this question in mind: Does the way in which people talk and write about works of art reflect something special or unique about the kinds of things they discuss? Can we discover in the work of art historians, critics, and theorists a way of distinguishing art from nonart?

It may seem strange to some readers that I wish to combine examples from art criticism, art history, and aesthetic theory in this chapter. Members of these various groups (critics, theorists, historians) sometimes insist that they have nothing to do with one another. Some aestheticians claim that in saying what art is they intend nothing about which things are good. Historians sometimes say that they neither evaluate nor define—simply classify and explain; that they are interested in particulars, not universals.

A historian of Greek art once told me that he believed that his students' reading Aristotle was not only a waste of time but positively harmful. His feelings are evidently similar to those formalist fears that talk about the content of work distracts one from the proper object of attention; Aristotle's writings may, presumably, tempt one away from the proper business of history. Museums, typically, do not hire or traffic with persons trained in aesthetics. (Friends of mine speak wistfully of the Cleveland Museum of Art as an outstanding exception to this rule.) In the United States, the membership of the Society for Aesthetics and Art Criticism consists mainly of professors of philosophy and English, occasionally a professional artist or critic, rarely a historian. However, I see no way ultimately of distinguishing the various aesthetic disciplines from one another. In deciding that a given object is worth interpreting, we evaluate. In giving a history of art we have to decide which objects we are going to give a history of, and we must thus have at least a working definition of 'art'.

Let us begin by looking at two passages that are typical of the sort of thing we find in discussions of art. One deals with "Eight O'Clock," a poem by A. E. Housman,[4] and the other with *The Raft of the Medusa*, a painting by Théodore Géricault. Here is Housman's poem:

Eight O'Clock

He stood, and heard the steeple
    Sprinkle the quarters on the morning town.
One, two, three, four, to market-place and people
    It tossed them down.

Strapped, noosed, nighing his hour,
    He stood and counted them and cursed his luck;
And then the clock collected in the tower
    Its strength, and struck.

And here is a typical critical discussion:

The impact of this poem is truly terrific. Its force is intensified by the sharpest possible contrast in rhythm between the scattered tinkling diversity of the second line and the slow forceful beat of the first half of the third line. This contrast is intensified in the second stanza and is brought to a climax in the deliberate, wavelike build-up of weight in the last two lines. The effect is redoubled by the suspenseful pause after "strength," followed by the final heavy blow at the very end. . . .

The voice we hear speaking in *Eight O'Clock* is that of a narrator who is very closely in sympathy with the psychological state of the doomed man. He feels the pressure of time weighing on him, and is aware of the irony in the fact that the clock itself seems to the doomed man to be the agent of his death. The impact would not be so great were it not that the beat, or rhythm, of the poem goes on in two ways at once. There is the effect of the contrasts, the suspense and gathering, and the final blow built up by the individual, dramatic manner of the presentation; and there is also the basic conventional pattern of the form the poet has chosen—the four-line stanza with alternating rhymes, and with a basic iambic pattern of alternating light and heavy stresses: "He stood, and heard the steeple . . ." Not all the syllables alternate so regularly, but this is the predominant pattern; and when, as in the second, third, and fifth lines, we find other variations, we can feel them pulling against this pattern to create a special emphasis. So also, each stanza begins with a line of three feet; the second and third lines have five feet, and the fourth, after this effect of expansion, contracts sharply to two. Meaningful variation within a pattern, and the use of skillfully contrived forms to suggest the sound of real speech, are signs of poetic craftsmanship.[5]

Consider too, the sorts of things the Géricault critic calls our attention to: (see plate I):

The brightest light falls from a patch of sky at the upper left of the picture. Its luminous blue is shot through with faint yellow. A touch of rose along the edges of the cloud near the top of the sail announces the imminent rise of the sun from behind a mass of clouds, through which it has begun to send a dark orange glow. Behind the Raft, at the left, rises an enormous wave, glassily transparent at the crest, its base a chasm of deepest green. Set against wave and sky, the Raft's sail has the colour of tanned leather, yellowish on the side of the light, a warm brown in the faintly translucent shadows. Farther to the right, the sky casts its strongest light, yellow mixed with silvery blue, over the dark figures at the mast; farther still, the sky turns to a bluish grey. The bronze torso of the signalling Negro jutting into the sky divides its areas of light and dark, his solid bulk causes the air spaces around him to recede into a vapoury distance. No less solid than this figure, the flank of a wave, bottle-green and veined with white, swells against the right edge of the picture.[6]

What happens as we read these comments? The most obvious effect of such criticism is that we come to pay closer attention to properties of the individual works. We are aware of the rhythm of "Eight O'Clock" to some extent the very first time we read it, just as we cannot help but notice that *The Raft of the Medusa* has colors. But these authors, in describing these works in detail, direct our attention to specific things that we may very well have overlooked before. We check to see what the rhythmic variations are in the second, third, and fifth lines. We look to see if the sail is a combination of tanned leather, yellow, and warm brown.

In *The Italian Painters of the Renaissance*, Bernhard Berenson poses the following question: "What is the point at which ordinary pleasures pass over into the specific pleasures derived from each one of the arts?"[7] We can ask this interesting question in more specific ways. When do the pleasures we derive from a good story pass over into the pleasures derived from literature? Or how does the delight felt in the presence of charming colors differ from that felt in the presence of a painting by Miró? It is not so much that critics increase our pleasure (although I believe they often do), as it is that they make that pleasure more specific. As Gombrich notes, "Critics . . . know how to use words to articulate their sensations and they let us profit in our own sensibility by teaching us differentiations."[8] While or after reading the above passages, we "pass over" from a general pleasure derived from the poem or painting to the specific pleasure derived from knowing more about how specific effects are achieved.

If the most important part of the institution of art is that related to talking about art, and the most important function of that talk is to bring about the sharing of experiences, the function of artistic discussion is, then, to bring people to see and hear features of objects which may go unnoticed. As we look at the examples of critical writings presented in this chapter, the reader will, I hope, come to discover the truth of this claim. We shall then be in a position to see how this function of criticism is related to the essential nature of art.

But we must also pay attention to another question: *How* do critics get us to notice intrinsic properties of works which we might not have noticed without their help? In the critical examples above, the authors point to properties of works that are there to be directly perceived, even though we may overlook or not notice them. But it is a mistake to think that critics simply direct us to the relevant surface details of a work of art. Often, too, they focus our attention on more abstract—though still intrinsic—properties. Sometimes these properties are so abstract as to be nearly impossible to perceive until we have been taught a special vocabulary. Even common terms such as 'balance' or 'form' or 'rhythm' can be troublesome, and require explanation. And words like 'chiaroscuro', 'inscape', or 'appoggiatura', words special to individual art forms, point out things which necessitate the same kind of study that is required when one masters a specialized scientific vocabulary. The claim that

> The minor version of 1–(2)–(3)–(4)–5–6–5, confining itself to the two basic "grievous" notes of the scale in a triadic context, clearly expresses a powerful assertion of fundamental unhappiness—the "protest" of 1–3–5 being extended into the "anguish" of 5–6–5[9]

will leave a reader unfamiliar with musical terminology befuddled rather than illuminated.

Critics and historians do, then, point to things in a work which we might not have seen, either because we did not look closely enough, or because we did not know what to look for. But they also point to, or point out, things *not in the work* at all. As an example, consider the kinds of topics an art historian—Bernhard Berenson—considers relevant to a thorough analysis of Italian Renaissance painters. In his highly regarded text *(The Italian Painters of the Renaissance)*, Berenson provides a running outline of his main topics. Although lengthy, a list of topics from the chapter on Venetian painting is instructive: the Venetians' use of color, the Church and painting, the spirit of the Renaissance, worship of greatness, study of ancient art, passion for glory, attitude to painting, love of pageantry, the Renaissance in Venice, love of comfort and splendor, painting as a common tongue, Venetians' passion for glory, gorgeous function, pageant pictures, state patronage in Venice, state patronage in Florence, painting and the confraternities, Carpaccio, Crivelli, Venetian culture, easel pictures, Giorgione, Catena, the portrait, sculpture and medals, Donatello, Pisanello, the new portraiture, choice of subjects, Giorgione's followers, Titian, the assunta, the late Renaissance in Venice, Lotto, spread of Spanish influence, the triumph of Spain, Titian, Titian's greatness, the old Titian, Tintoretto, the experiment of Eclecticism, Tintoretto, light and shadow, Tintoretto's religious sense, conception of human form, value of minor episodes, Tintoretto's *Crucifixion*, Tintoretto's portraits, the Venetian provinces, Paolo Veronese, life in Verona, love of the countryside, Palma Vecchio, Bonifazio Veronese, Jacopo Bassano, success of the Bassani, Bassano's treatment of light, the first modern landscapes, the Venetians and Velázquez, the Epigoni, the later Venice, Longhi, Canaletto, Guardi, Tiepolo, the death of Venetian painting.[10] Berenson covers an incredibly broad range of topics in his attempt to tell the reader, "whence it came from and what it led to." As Berenson himself comments, we more fully appreciate an object when we are given this kind of contextual information.[11]

I have claimed that critics, historians, and aestheticians get us to focus in certain ways on specific objects. And they often do this, as Berenson does, by referring to features of the context of the work, as well as to things about the work itself. In the rest of this chapter we shall look at some examples of references to extrinsic or contextual properties of works of art, and we shall consider the extent to which these properties can be used to form an adequate theory of art. I shall argue that none, taken singly, can provide an adequate theory, but that considered as a group they can lead us to a way of distinguishing art from nonart.

The classification I put forth here is in some ways reminiscent of Aristotle's four causes. Aristotle believed that complete understanding of anything entailed answering four questions: "Who made it?" "What is it made of?" "What is its form?" and "Why was it made?" I shall not add to the considerable discussion that has centered on the nature and adequacy of these four "causes." What Aristotle was right about is the fact that we approach objects with a curiosity that seeks to discover a great many things about them. What those things are will depend upon ourselves, the object, and the situation. Satisfaction results only when a variety of things are discovered, some of them having to do with the object in and of itself, some of them with things outside of the object. My reasons for choosing the categories below will become clearer in later chapters. For now, suffice it to say that I intend to concentrate on questions which frequently arise in discussions of art, and in particular in the attempt to understand art objects.

Aristotle's question "What is its form?" would lead us to focus attention on intrinsic properties of the kind we have already considered: an object's shape, color, texture, or size. Although no "natural" classification of the extrinsic topics critics cover is obvious, we can borrow from and add to the list of questions that Aristotle said we must be able to answer if we can be said to comprehend something adequately.

1. What kind(s) of activity or craft was involved in the production of the object? Answering this question usually consists of explaining the artist's media and methods, and I label it "Artistic Activity."

2. What kind of person made it? This question follows directly from the first question, for understanding an activity always entails knowing something about the agent performing the actions. There are a great many different questions asked under this category: what the artist's "roots" (training, or history) were, for example, or what he or she was like psychologically. I shall deal with this sort of question under the general heading "The Artist's Life."

3. What are the intentions with which the object was made? Clearly this question is closely related to the first two and only separated off from them arbitrarily. This is particularly true when we ask what artistic or technical problems the artist was trying to solve. However, the general question of the extent to which knowing an artist's intentions is relevant to the understanding of his or her work has been so widely and lengthily discussed in criticism and aesthetics that I have devoted a separate section, "Artistic Intentions," to it.

4. What does the object describe or express? This question differs from those given above and below in that, unlike them, it cannot be asked of all objects. (Or at least of every artifact. See chapter 4 for a discussion of artifactuality as a condition of art.) At least some works of art, unlike rocks and light bulbs, have a "content." They are "about" something or "express" something and do this through various sorts of symbol systems. A great deal of critical writing deals with this aspect of art objects. I have thus included a section entitled "The Content of a Work of Art."

5. What is the function of the object? To what use or uses is it put? So-called instrumental theories of art assert that it is the special function of works of art which separates them from other objects; others have argued that the lack of function is what makes art objects special. We shall, in the section entitled "The Function of a Work of Art," look briefly at both claims, and consider ways in which function figures in discussions of works of art.

6. How does the object fit into its sociocultural setting? How does a work of art affect, and how is it affected by, this setting? Anthropological, sociological, and political investigations of art are more and more frequent, as are positions which have as a pivotal point the consideration of art as an institution. We shall examine this question in section vii, "The Setting of a Work of Art."

The positions referred to in these sections are well known to people familiar with aesthetics and the philosophy of criticism. All of them have been discussed widely, from a variety of viewpoints. Each is deserving of far more detailed attention than it receives here. There is a sense in which my treatment may be unsatisfying to everyone: people who are familiar with them will find little new; people unfamiliar, and for whom I include this as an introduction, will find too much that is new. But readers are asked to remember that the discussion is intended to show one thing crucial to the argument developed in the rest of the book. Theorists have attempted to construct definitions of 'works of art' based upon the kinds of issues critics return to again and again in their analyses. As we shall see, none of these definitions is satisfactory. Yet the things critics stress still seem to be central to an understanding of art. Readers are also asked to bear in mind the suggestion that investigating how art is discussed may tell us something about its nature, and this demands considerable exposure to what goes on when people talk about works of art. Even sophisticated readers may thus benefit from looking at the examples that follow, and by being reminded of some of the problems they exemplify.

We began this chapter with the hunch that what happens when we discuss works of art is that we come to see more in those works than we would have seen without discussion, and we are about to test this claim further, by looking at more specific examples of criticism. However, we must make this hypothesis clearer before we begin testing it, and this requires a fuller analysis of the function of criticism. If we can agree that the function of criticism (or at least a primary function) is to illuminate works by bringing us to a fuller perception of them, we will be on our way to a definition of 'work of art'; the definition would include as a necessary condition that a 'work of art' be that which can be talked about in this manner. And if *what* we perceive as a consequence of this kind of critical discussion can be restricted, perhaps we shall also get a sufficient condition.

There are, I think, two other candidates for the primary function of criticism: *(a)* the evaluation of a work of art and *(b)* the proof that a work of art is good or bad. By *(a)* I mean evaluation "pure and simple," where someone simply says that a work of art is wonderful or that he or she likes or dislikes it. "I love, I even adore *War and Peace* . . ." said Constantine Leontiev.[12] But if this sort of expression were the essential nature or function of criticism, we should assign it the same degree of significance we give to individuals' reports on how much or little they like carrots or raw oysters. Of course critics do give evaluations, and even when they don't explicitly mention their adoration, we usually assume that they wouldn't bother to talk about works they didn't value to some extent. But the interest we have comes from our desire to know *why* someone adores *War and Peace*, so that we concentrate on the way Leontiev finishes his sentence: "for being a gigantic work for its bold introduction into the novel of whole sections of philosophy and strategy contrary to rules of artistic restraint and accuracy that have governed us for so long."[13]

But, we must ask ourselves, does the interest then derive from our desire for a proof (function [*b*])? Is it the main function of criticism to present valid argumentation in support of the claim that a particular work is worthy of adoration? There are those who believe that this is the case, that pointing to such things as "sections of philosophy and strategy" is a means of rationally persuading others to share feelings about a work. Thus C. J. Ducasse says, "The statement that a given work possesses a certain objective characteristic expresses at the same time a judgment of value if the characteristic is one that the judging person approves, or as the case may be, disapproves, and is thus one that he regards as conferring, respectively, positive or negative value on any object of the given kind that happens to possess it."[14]

Arnold Isenberg discusses this way of looking at art criticism in an influential article, "Critical Communication,"[15] and I wish to elaborate on that discussion here. Rationality consists in being able to state reasons for our beliefs or actions. One way in which we might understand giving a reason in support of a claim is according to the following model: A claim is made, a reason is given in support of the claim, and a lawlike generalization is forthcoming that relates the claim and the reason. Thus:

Smith: It's cold out today. (Claim)
Jones: How do you know?
Smith: Because I can see the exhaust vapor from all the cars that pass by. (Reason)

Smith's second statement counts as a *reason* for his claim (and will similarly count as a reason for Jones's acceptance of it) only if there is a lawlike

generalization relating them, such as, "Whenever you can see exhaust from all
the cars that pass by it is (probably) cold." This is a case in which the claim
and reason are related by an inductive generalization. Our reasons for beliefs
can also, of course, be the result of deductive reasoning.

> Smith: Those two triangles are congruent.
> Jones: Why?
> Smith: Because they have two corresponding equal sides and the angles
> formed by those two sides are equal.

Here Smith's statements are held together by the "Side/Angle/Side" theorem
of plane geometry.

Isenberg calls statements in a critical model similar to the above "verdict,"
"reason," and "norm."

> Smith: *War and Peace* is wonderful. (Verdict)
> Jones: Why?
> Smith: Because it has moving depictions of battles. (Reason)

Again, in order for Smith's second statement to count as a reason, there must
exist a lawlike generalization or norm, namely, "Novels with moving descriptions of battles are wonderful."

Is this model appropriate to criticism? And if, as I am inclined to believe, it
is not appropriate, can we view criticism as a rational activity? One might
insist that Jones's "Why?" here is out of place—"I just like it, don't ask me
why"—and then criticism would simply be a stating of one's preferences. If
indeed the business of criticism is to state such preferences, critical commentary should be analogous to other statements of one's likes or dislikes:

> Smith: I like raw carrots.
> Jones: Why?

How should Smith respond? Perhaps he shouldn't—should instead simply
say, "I just like them, I don't know why, so don't ask me." But suppose he is
willing to do more than simply state a preference and tries to explain himself.

> Smith: Because they taste good.

If Smith here has given a reason on something of a par with "Because I can see
the exhaust," or "Because they have two corresponding equal sides and the
angles between those sides are equal," then there must be a generalization
which links it with the statement that he likes raw carrots. But surely "If

things taste good, I like them," is a tautology and hence "Because they taste good" isn't a *reason* but a restatement of "I like them."

Let's try again.

Smith: Because they're crunchy.

Perhaps we do now have a genuine inductive generalization at work: "If foods are crunchy, I (Smith) tend(s) to like them." But suppose Jones now says, "Do you?" Must Smith *believe* that the generalization he has just uttered (or some other one, "I tend to like yellow vegetables," "I tend to like things high in vitamins") is true *before* he claims to like carrots? In the inductive and deductive examples above, our belief in the claims made depends upon our belief in some supporting generalization. But it seems absurd to maintain that our liking of certain foods waits upon our formulating and verifying supporting generalizations. Thus it seems that that model is inappropriate here.

If liking *War and Peace* is like liking carrots, the model will be inappropriate there as well. Perhaps this lies behind the often heard remark "I don't know much about art, but I do know what I like." Liking seems not to depend upon the formulation and verification of generalizations.

There may be a way, however, in which this model does fit both criticism and food preferences. Generalizations that tie reasons and claims together not only provide for explanation, they also allow for prediction. If it is cold outside, I expect to see exhaust steam. We do seem to be able to make predictions about preferences for food and art. We can predict that family and friends will like foods they've never tasted, or music they've never heard. And once we've gotten "to know" film critics, for example, we can predict that we will like or dislike what they like. There must at least be something like inductive generalizations at work here.

I have said that rationality entails being prepared to give reasons for acting or believing as we do. In the examples above, the reasons Smith gives in support of his claims are related by a law. But there are other ways in which people give a rationale for what they do. For example, sometimes people explain their actions as being in accord with principles or commitments.

Smith: I have to return this book to the library.
Jones: Why?
Smith: Because people should always return things that they borrow.

Yet it is difficult to see how our preferences for food or books can be subsumed under this model of providing a rationale. One may, because of principles one has, try to develop one's tastes. But surely it is incorrect to suggest that

anyone likes raw carrots or *War and Peace* because he or she has a principle
requiring him to do so.

The existence of these difficulties could lead us to conclude that reason
giving is totally superfluous in criticism or to suspect that the role of reason
giving in criticism is simply not the same as it is in those models where claims
are tied to laws or principles. The latter is the step—the correct one, I
believe—that Isenberg finally recommends, and it leads to a kind of middle
ground between *(a)* and *(b)*. He insists that the verdict-reason-norm model
does not capture the essence of criticism. It is not because norms are not
discoverable in this area, for the business of criticism does not depend on
that. Rather it is because the utterance of reason-giving statements has as its
function something entirely different from giving reasons in support of ver-
dicts. Instead, the role of critics is to bring about a fuller perception of the
works they discuss. As Isenberg explains,

> The critic's meaning is "filled in," "rounded out," "completed," by the act
> of perception, which is performed not to judge the truth of his description
> but in a certain sense to *understand* it. And if *communication* is a process
> by which a mental content is transmitted by symbols from one person to
> another, then we can say that it is a function of criticism to bring about
> communication at the level of the sense, that is, to induce a sameness of
> vision of experienced content. If this is accomplished, it may or may not be
> followed by agreement, or what is called "communion"—a community of
> feeling which expresses itself in identical value judgments.[16]

Paul Ziff also argues that critical activity does not essentially consist in
proving that a given work is good or bad. Believing that 'good' roughly means
'worth contemplating,' he says that anything that counts as a reason for a
thing's being good must also count as a reason for its being worth contemplating. Hence, reasons must *invite* contemplation. Any invitation to contemplation carries with it an assumption that others will care about what is there to be
contemplated.[17] But not all people care about the same things; so what is a
reason for me to contemplate something will not necessarily be a reason for
you. This may explain why I can make predictions about all (or most) cars'
exhaust vapor on cold days, but am limited to making predictions about
culinary or artistic preference of only people whom I know rather well. At best
we have "reasons for me" or "my group" and these are not adequate for *proofs*
which require that things are *in general* reasons.

Both Isenberg and Ziff give us a basis for rejecting *(b)* above as the main
function of criticism, for it seems that the attempt to give reasons in support of
our evaluations is pointless. Even if I give you what look or sound like reasons

for eating spinach, I will not conclude that you are *irrational* if you don't then like it, too, in the way that I do have grounds for thinking you irrational if you deny that it is cold in the face of a lot of automobile exhaust vapor. I can point to moving battle depictions in *War and Peace*, but will not conclude that you are being irrational if you don't then like the book. But if it is not unreasonable to continue disliking *War and Peace* no matter what I point to in explanation of my opinion that it is worth contemplating, then my statements cannot be *reasons* at all; they are merely pointings.

The activity of criticism is very complex and it is unlikely that it can be distinguished, in terms of either goal or methodology, from all other scientific activity or from mere statements of preference or from mathematical reasoning or from everyday observation. However, we have seen no compelling reason yet to reject *bringing viewers to a fuller perception* of a work as a candidate for the primary function of criticism. As we now turn to specific examples of the way in which critics, historians, and theorists talk about works of art in an attempt to discover in them a basis for distinguishing art from nonart, readers should also consider whether they, like me, find that criticism does indeed function in this fashion.

ii. Artistic Activity

If there were a way of distinguishing artistic activity from all other kinds of activity, then we would certainly be well on our way to distinguishing art from nonart. A "yes" or "no" answer to the question "Was this thing produced through or by artistic activity?" would settle the matter. But do we believe that we can make this distinction? If a poet and a botanist go together into a field of daisies, can we tell which is which by looking at what they do? Do we, or can we, distinguish a poem from a botanical treatise in terms of the different actions performed by their producers?

Historically, it has often been assumed that artistic objects are the products of a special kind of activity, an activity that can specifically be called "artistic." That is, it has been assumed that artistic activity differs in some fundamental way or ways from other kinds of activities. For Plato, the problem of defining art was that of seeing how it compared to and contrasted with other sorts of craft, the upshot being that he dubbed all imitative art as only "pseudo-craft." According to him, artists follow no rational or intelligible plan. They engage in purely intuitive or emotional activity, proceeding not from an acquired skill, but simply from an inspiration not unlike madness. What they do is not rule-governed, nor can it be taught.

Later theorists were favorably inclined toward viewing the artist as a genuine craftsman. Artists in the Middle Ages and Renaissance belonged to what were essentially labor or trade unions and were certainly thought to be skilled artisans. Sculptors were stonecutters (the word for both is still the same in some languages, e.g., 'hugger' in Danish), and architects were engineers. And in the eighteenth century, theorists emphasized a combination in an artist of skilled technique and artistic inspiration.

The controversy as to whether artistic activity is primarily emotional or cognitive remains unsettled. What is indisputable and important for our purposes here is that what artists do as they create their poems and pictures has been, and continues to be, of tremendous interest to critics, historians, and theorists.

There are, certainly, many actions that we associate closely with the production of works of art. Some associate fairly directly and uniquely, others more loosely. We could imagine playing a game called "What's being made or done?" in which we are given short descriptions of acts and are then to answer the question which is the title of the game. The immediate answer to "putting paint on canvas with a brush" would be "(making a) painting"; to "moving across a stage on tiptoe," "ballet dancing." But there will be more hesitation with "hacking away at a stone," and even more with "sitting at a typewriter." Even in the less troublesome cases, the actions do not serve as necessary and sufficient conditions for the activity with which they are associated. One can, after all, paint a tent or sneak across a stage.

Our inability to distinguish art from nonart on the basis of a special kind of activity engaged in by those who produce the former but not by those who produce the latter has been intensified in our century. Paint is thrown, typewriters are sat upon, cellos are chopped up. While walking in Battersea Park in September 1977, my nephew and I saw men putting colored sheets of plastic on the ground. (See plate II.) It was not until we read a sign announcing an art exhibit that we realized that they were engaged in artistic activity—and indeed even then we were not wholly convinced. Might they not have been park groundsmen preparing the area for the show? A rough distinction between "made by a person" and "made by a machine" can be drawn, perhaps. Thus an object that has been chiseled from some material—rock or soap—is more likely to qualify as art than one which comes from a plastic mold. However, often both artists and nonartists use the same tools and machines—a blow torch, for example. When the Picasso statue in Chicago's City Center was being erected, several people refused to let it be attributed to the master because he himself never came to Chicago. The work was done by metal workers. Isn't there a difference, it was asked, between Picasso's plans and an engineer's plans?

Furthermore, descriptions as general as "putting paint on canvas with a brush" are not the sort found in the writings of art historians and critics and do not give the kind of help those writers seek to provide. Of course, someone who has never heard of Géricault will be helped a bit when informed "he put paint on canvas with a brush." But that remark will not explain the critic's preferences or help us to have a fuller perception of one of Géricault's works. Thus the comments critics make concerning craft or technique are always of a much more limited sort—"the sentences this author uses are usually no longer than six words," "this painter uses subdued colors," or "this composer favors minor keys." Hence we find the following kinds of statements about the artists' craft:

> Prosaically minded people, from Palomino onwards, have asserted that Velasquez must have used exceptionally long brushes, but the brushes he holds in the Meninas are of normal length.[18]

or:

> Except for the pallid light imparting an ashen hue to Christ and the Mourners in [El Greco's] Crucifixion, the terrible desolation is not conveyed by physical horrors. . . . The misery is transmitted to the Virgin, St. John and the impassioned Magdalene. The light flickering across the forms accentuates the nervous agitation of pose, drapery or gesture. The effect is curiously fluid, recalling El Greco's habit of modelling his figures in wax prior to painting them. This was quite a common practice, but no other artist exploited the molten quality of the wax in his final translation of the idea into paint. It accorded well with his strange elongated proportions, which allied to the sameness of all his faces endows his sacred themes with a haunting timelessness, at once remote and immediate.[19]

Often critics point, in addition, to more general problems faced by groups of artists. Thus Berenson emphasizes the importance of touch in adding a third dimension to sight, something common, obviously, to all of the visual arts:

> . . . the essential in the art of painting . . . is somehow to stimulate our consciousness of tactile values, so that the picture shall have at least as much power as the objects represented, to appeal to our tactile imaginations.[20]

Failing to know this, a viewer may well miss much of the particular mastery of Giotto.

Similarly, other critics focus on special techniques artists develop and use in order to solve special problems. One special set of problems, for example, confronted architects of ancient Greek temples, for they were faced with alluvial soil and frequent earthquakes. One expert explains:

> The traditional Greek method of building was well designed to meet these rather awkward conditions, for the foundations of a Greek temple are in effect a raft: every block is joined by metal clamps to every other block, so that the whole platform is a unity.[21]

Those who know something about engineering will appreciate the skills of an architect. Knowing something about the location of a building will augment our understanding of why it was designed the way it was.

A broader set of questions which critics sometimes pose deals with general claims about genres or movements. Discussing the genre of modern dance, Rudolf Arnheim claims:

> The modern dance has run into an interesting inner conflict by stressing the weight of the human body—which the classical ballet had tried to deny— and at the same time following the general trend in moving from realistic pantomime to abstraction.[22]

And Michael Fried observes that the modern painter

> has come to find it imperative that it [painting] defeat or suspend its own objecthood, and that the crucial factor in this undertaking is shape which must belong to *painting*—it must be pictorial, not literal.[23]

These claims are typical of critical explanations which focus on problems confronting an individual artist or genre, period, or school of art. The problems facing an artist will have a tremendous effect on his or her activity. If we mistake a chiseled object for one that has been modeled, we will not understand it; we will look for things which are not there and miss things that are.

This is one of the reasons that we must risk the danger of being distracted, a danger that accompanies permission to refer to extrinsic as well as intrinsic properties. If one expects all painting to be naturalistic, much, if not all, is lost when one looks at the work of ancient Egyptian painters, or at Byzantine mosaics.

These kinds of critical comments do, then, prod us into taking a closer look, or into looking from a different angle. But art cannot be distinguished from nonart on the basis of the craft or technique which went into its production. The mere fact that an object was produced in a certain way does not insure its being a work of art. As we saw above, a description of the activity involved—say, "put paint on canvas" or "used long brushes"—will not provide necessary and/or sufficient conditions. People other than artists do this, and the notion of 'painting' has been broadened to include the placement of material other than paint on material other than canvas with things other than brushes.

But another more important reason that art cannot be distinguished from nonart solely on the basis of the technique or craft involved follows from Weitz's arguments for the nondefinability of 'art'. He believed, it will be recalled (see chapter 1), that the creative aspects of artistic activity preclude the defining of the term. While I do not accept this completely, I do think he is right with respect to artistic technique. In all of the arts, the ways in which individuals go about their work are constantly undergoing developments and changes. New tools are invented as are new methods for using them. We are currently witnessing the development of new artistic techniques based upon the use of computers and other electronic devices. There is also much experimentation with combining art-forms, photography and poetry for example. Carl-Erik Ström's photograph of a man looking out over a sea is accompanied by the words:

Denna man ser sent i sitt liv for första gangen ut over ett stort hav. Just i denna stund bestammer han sig for att skaffa sig en bot.

(This man looks, late in life across a large sea for the first time. Exactly at that moment he decides to get a boat.)

The words and the image form a new whole. (See figure 5.)

Any definition of art based upon a description of what artists do and have done will be unable to predict what artists may do in the future. And I believe it is equally difficult to think of cases of kinds of actions which we feel intuitively that it is incorrect to dub "artistic." Strange as it may appear, men laying out yards of plastic is not in and of itself unartistic. One could, of course, arbitrarily close off the possibilities, but to do so would be to blind oneself to one feature of the creativity which is essential to art.

iii. The Artist's Life

The failure of the attempt to account for what art is in terms of the overt activity in which artists engage accounts, at least in part, for the fact that theorists often turn from overt to covert facts about artists. Instead of limiting the discussion to what kind of thing is being done, we find attempts to explain art in terms of the kind of person doing it. Here we must ask whether the

Fig. 5. Carl-Erik Ström, *Man Looking Out to Sea*; from "Calle's Art," in Carl-Erik Ström's *The Mighty Photographer*; published by Tryckerigruppen, Malmo, Sweden, 1979.

distinction between art and nonart follows from the fact that artists form a unique class of people, or whether in their biographies there is some clue which will permit us to distinguish the sorts of things they produce from nonartistic objects.

Historians and critics do, certainly, provide us with a great deal of personal information about artists. Sometimes it is something about the temperament or attitude of the artist that is deemed important. Consider this typical discussion of an artist's temperament:

> If we judge [Masolino's works] by the same standards that we apply to those of Masaccio, then Masolino is definitely the loser. . . . [T]he temperaments of these two artists were completely different, not to say conflicting. . . . Obviously, quite apart from the difference of subject [of Masolino's *Temptation of Adam and Eve* and Masaccio's *Expulsion of Adam and Eve from the Garden of Eden*], it is futile to compare this [subtle gracefulness] with the expressive impulsiveness of Masaccio, since, if we do so, it will seem

lifeless, whereas it is in reality extremely vivacious, though in a different way.[24]

And note this analysis of Hardy's "melancholy view" of the world:

Hardy's was a speculative mind, instinctively reasoning from particular observations to a general conclusion. Since the world he looked at seemed so full of pain and disappointment, then, he argued, pain and disappointment were outstanding characteristics of human existence. . . . This disposition to a melancholy view was confirmed and increased by the age in which he lived.[25]

Or consider this discussion of Bartók's personal psychology:

Knowledge concerning Bartók's own feelings of isolation in the years surrounding "Mandarin's" creation leaves no doubt that he has projected essential features of his own psychological, political and social make-up into the ballet's title-role and its strange fate—one against all, mortal but at the same time unwounded in its fundamental human vitality.[26]

Another common critical practice is to attempt to explain an aesthetic object by referring to something unique about its creator's history. Sometimes this consists of pointing to something about the artist's individual background, his or her training, perhaps, in an effort to explain something about the work. For example, Guido Ballo insists that one can only understand El Greco (see plate III) if one realizes that his training was Byzantine and not Venetian. It is wrong, he believes, to compare him with Titian, for this can never explain the atonality of his work.[27]

Critics refer, even, to particular events in an artist's life by way of explaining his or her work. Thus Maria Shirley comments:

During the sack of Rome, Cellini energetically defended the city against the forces of Charles V. Ironically, he was later accused of having stolen priceless jewelry during the fighting, and in 1537 he was imprisoned in the Castel Sant' Angelo, where his deprivations caused a series of visionary experiences. This intense religious feeling inspired the life-size crucifix, which was originally intended for his own tomb.[28]

Another example is Kenneth Clark's discussion of Goya's personal history:

In 1792 Goya had a serious illness which left him totally deaf. . . . Gesture and facial expression, when they are seen without the accompanying sound, become unnaturally void. . . .[29]

Or consider Shirley's comments on the details of El Greco's life:

> The failure of this picture [El Greco's *The Martyrdom of St. Maurice*] to win
> the king's favor determined the subsequent course of Greco's career in
> Spain. Debarred from court patronage, he turned his attention to ecclesias-
> tical admirers of his strange imagination. The discrepancies of scale be-
> tween the foreground and the middle distance, the off-centre composition,
> the rhetorical poses and elongated proportions are part of the general legacy
> of Italian Mannerism, but he combines them in a special way, which allied
> to the cool yet vivid colour, creates a mood of supernatural intensity.[30]

In this last example, we see a shift from an attempt to explain El Greco's
work in terms of details from his personal psychology or biography to an
explanation by comparison with a school or style of art. Criticism is almost
always explicitly or implicitly comparative in nature, so that even when particular incidents of an artist's life are described, the intention is comparative;
the details are explained in such a way that a critic can relate the unique
individual background of the artist to the general historical setting into which
he or she is placed. And these comparisons are the fundamental tools of
history, criticism, and theory. Properties of individual works often will not be
noticed unless the work is perceived as a part of, or as a reaction against, a
particular tradition. Gombrich has commented on the importance of this kind
of comparative writing:

> It is the appreciation of the artist's choice and of the skill with which he
> carries out his decisions that forms an essential part of what we mean by
> understanding a work. Take the proverbial apples by Cézanne. Surely those
> who merely compare them in their minds with apples seen at the green
> grocers will not derive much solace or edification. It is rather by comparing
> them with standard still-life apples that we find in the master's single-
> minded concentration on their shapes rather than on their texture a symp-
> tom of his attitude to life, his dogged search for essentials.[31] (See figure 6)

One artist's work is better understood by comparing it to the work of another
artist, or by comparing the works of the same artist with one another, as when
Berenson tells us:

> The difference between the old Titian . . . and the young Titian, painter of
> the *Assumption*, and of the *Bacchus and Ariadne*, is the difference between
> the Shakespeare of the *Midsummer's Night Dream* and the Shakespeare of
> *The Tempest*.[32]

Finally, critics often discuss artists within the even broader context of the

Fig. 6. Paul Cézanne, *The Plate of Apples.* **Collection of The Art Institute of Chicago.**

whole of artistic history or provide us with the general historic context in which particular art works appear. T. S. Eliot, for example, argues in his famous essay, "Tradition and the Individual Talent," that poets' creations are determined by, and in turn determine, the interpretation of those of their predecessors.[33] When a critic or historian explicates the historic context of a work, we are then in a position to know how to approach it. In a recent exhibit by the Danish artist Bjørn Nørgård, a row of busts with stuffed pigheads was set under a white arch. (See figure 7.) The busts were on columns where the names of well-known political personalities also appeared, and on the columns of the arches were photos of marble portrait busts by Thorvaldsen. Knowing something about the tradition of sculpting busts of famous persons gives us some handle on this exhibit. But it is a rare viewer indeed who does not feel grateful for this further explanation:

Fig. 7. Bjørn Nørgard, *Pig Heads on Pedestals*. Kunstmuseum Luzern.

[The eighteenth-century Danish sculptor] Thorvaldsen created during his
lifetime a great number of marble-busts of significant princes. According to
the demands of art at that time, it was not most important to create a
resemblance between the portrait and the real person. The idealization was
conspicuous. But so one also achieved a possibility of replacement. Seen
from a historical point of view, it has actually no more importance who is
supposed to be who. Connecting stuffed pigheads with political personalities, the artist draws his attention to the changeableness of the idea of
power-politics, in whom and in which time may be personified. The persons
who are indicated by names have primarily a substitutional function.[34]

Objections to this kind of criticism generally concentrate on the danger of
its directing attention to the maker rather than to the thing made. Wellek and
Warren express this fear in the following way:

The biographical approach actually obscures a proper comprehension of the
literary process, since it breaks up the order of literary tradition to substitute the life cycle of an individual.[35]

I do not at all share this attitude. Shirley's essay, for example, might be read
by someone interested only in the gossip connected with El Greco's life, and

such a reader might take greater satisfaction in finding out that the King of Spain did not like his painting than in his art's special qualities. But that certainly is not the critic's fault. Consider a further example of her elegant criticism:

> Greco's eye reacted to the stimulus of color with unusual alacrity and sensibility. Spain transformed his colour in two ways at once, releasing his palette from the conventional richness of Venetian hues, and investing it with colour harmonies which were at once intensely personal and expressive. Obviously Greco's first impressions of the land counted for much; above all the painful contests between spring and winter which characterized the landscape around him in late March: the silvery green of wild myrtle, thyme, and rosemary, the snowy peaks of the steel-gray Guadarramas, and the sparsely-cultivated plateau revealing strips of ploughed red earth edged with trees whose foliage is of such painful green that they resemble daggers piercing the skyline. Finally there are the skies, where the clear sapphire air is suddenly obscured by the charcoal darkness of the storm, rent only by clouds resembling tattered rags tossed about in the empty vastness. Greco alone has given pictorial expression to its wild elemental force, and perhaps just because he was a foreigner his eye registered its uniqueness with a peculiar vividness.[36]

What is important here is not merely that El Greco was a foreigner, but that as a foreigner he reacted in vivid ways to colors. Reading this, one's concentration on El Greco's use of color is intensified, not interrupted. And the fact that one may also look more closely at *Spain* is in no way inconsistent with this; it in no way undermines the validity of her comments on the original painting. (See plate III.)

It is not the worry that reference to an artist's life is distracting that constitutes the weakness here. It is, rather, that facts about the artist do not provide a foundation on which to rest the distinction between art and nonart. In fairness to the writers we have just looked at, we must remember that they are in no way claiming that they do provide such a foundation. Perhaps the theory that comes closest to distinguishing art from nonart comes from psychologists, in particular psychoanalysts, who claim that there is something psychologically unique about artists. If this were true, we could pick them out from all other people, and we would then have a de facto way of separating art and nonart.

Part of the appeal of this view comes, I think, from the fact that in our century people often seem to have little more that counts as evidence for an object's being a work of art than that the object was created by someone already identified as an artist. Thus if the orange crate in our original example had been placed in the sculpture garden by Picasso that would be one thing, quite another thing if put there by Sam the Gardener.

Freud was, of course, extremely interested in artists, as were and are many of his followers. But he never, as far as I know, took the extreme position (required if it is to be of help in solving our problem) that all, and only, people with a certain psychological makeup create art. Most psychoanalytic writing about art is an attempt to understand the artist through his or her work, sometimes vice versa, but almost never an attempt to understand art per se as the product of a certain kind of abnormal person. Ernest Jones's comment in "The Death of Hamlet's Father" is typical of so-called Freudian critics:

> When a poet takes an old theme from which to create a work of art, it is always interesting, and often instructive, to note the respects in which he changes elements in the story. Much of what we glean of Shakespeare's personality is derived from such studies, the direct biographical details being so sparse.[37]

People who approach art in this way are often criticized for committing what C. S. Lewis and E. M. W. Tillyard called the "personal heresy": using a work as a means of understanding the artist instead of considering the work on its own merits. In an essay on psychoanalysis and literary criticism, Lewis said that as long as the approach is understood as pathology—and not criticism— he had nothing against it:

> Unfortunately, however, we sometimes meet with a real confusion in which the proposition, "This poem is an inevitable outcome, and an illuminating symptom, of the poet's repressions" is somehow treated as an answer to the proposition "This poem is rubbish." The critic has allowed himself to be diverted from the genuinely critical question "Why, and how, should we read this?" to the purely historical question "Why did he write it?"—and that, too, in a sense which makes the word "why" mean not "with what intention" but "impelled by what causes?" He is asking not for the Final Cause, which would still have some literary importance, but for the Efficient, which has none.[38]

Jones comes closer to providing a way of distinguishing artists from non-artists in "The Problem of Paul Morphy," when he says,

> Genius is evidently the capacity to apply unusual gifts with intense, even if only temporary concentration. I would suggest that this, in its turn, depends on a special capacity for discovering conditions under which the unconscious guilt can be held in complete abeyance. This is doubtless to be

connected with the well-known rigour, the sincerity, and the purity of the artistic conscience. It is purchased, however, at the cost of psychical integrity being at the mercy of any disturbance of these indispensable conditions. And that would appear to be the seat of "artistic sensitiveness."[39]

Jones's argument here seems to be this: The production of a work of art requires an act of intense psychological concentration. This concentration is possible only when an individual is able to repress all guilt. People who must exert the extreme psychic energy required by this repression are easily "set off" by external disturbances or interruptions. That artists are in fact "temperamental" in exactly this way is supported by our knowledge of their erratic behavior. But notice that for our purposes this argument would be crucial (if true) only if all and only people who behave erratically produce works of art. But obviously (and unfortunately) that is not the case.

That a defining characteristic of artistic activity is not to be found in this kind of psychological approach is demonstrated in Freud's comparison of works of art and dreams. Both are products of phantasy-making activity; both require similar kinds of interpretation; and both result from subconscious attempts to repress sexual anxieties. But the connection between dreaming and producing art works would provide a basis for distinguishing art and nonart only if there were something *unique* about the dreaming of artists.

Freud believed that dreams and poems, like everything else, must have a cause. Those of us who believe that all events have causes will not disagree with him here. But that similar things necessarily have the same cause is not true and becomes more and more suspect as that similarity becomes less and less obvious. Even if we could be certain that a particular sexual trauma were the cause of a particular symbol's appearance in a dream, it would follow that that trauma accounted for the same symbol's appearance in a painting only if the symbols were actually identical, and, more crucially, only if dreams and paintings were the same kinds of things, which they clearly are not. The fact that one is private, mental, and involuntary and the other mainly public, physical, and voluntary destroys the analogy.

I shall not add here to the controversy surrounding psychoanalysis and its status or lack of status as a scientific theory.[40] Rather I shall borrow some questions raised by Wittgenstein in "Conversations on Freud." Wittgenstein thinks that Freud's explanations of the origins of dreams (and hence of artworks) have the same sort of appeal as do mythological explanations. We can see objects on a table in front of us as paralleling or symbolizing problems we face in our personal lives—for example, how the catsup bottle threatens the sugar bowl. So we can interpret (read into) our dreams in terms of our problems; and since as human beings we share many problems, we can interpret other people's dreams along the same lines:

> But dreaming—using this sort of language—although it *may* be used to refer to a woman or to a phallus, may *also* be used not to refer to that at all. If some activity is shown to be carried out often for a certain purpose— striking someone to inflict pain—then a hundred to one it is also carried out under other circumstances *not* for that purpose. He may just want to strike him without thinking of inflicting pain at all. The fact that we are inclined to recognize the hat as a phallic symbol does not mean that the artist was necessarily referring to a phallus in any way when she painted it.[41]

Further, he comments, it is as mistaken to believe that people have only one reason to create works of art as it would be to assume that people have only one reason to talk:

> Compare the question of why we dream and why we write stories. Not everything in the story is allegorical. What would be meant by trying to explain why he has written just that story in just that way?
>
> There is no one reason why people talk. A small child babbles often just for the pleasure of making noises. This is also one reason why adults talk. And there are countless others.[42]

Thus in positing the same cause and the same sort of interpretations for all works of art, psychoanalytic theorists actually weaken the explanatory force of their claims. The question "What is the garden doing *in this work?*" will not be satisfactorily answered if we only explain why gardens *generally* appear in dreams or artworks. The garden in a particular work may have the same cause as a garden in a man's dream, but not necessarily. Or it may have other causes, for example, artistic traditions, that are completely lacking in a little boy's dream.

The shortcomings of psychoanalytic theory can, for our purposes, be generalized to cover all of the things referred to by critics under the heading of "the artist's life." We are attempting to discover in this kind of critical writing a means for separating objects of art from nonart. This would only be possible here if artists (and hence what they make) had in their life something which made them distinct from nonartists. But temperament, training, history, biography, though they may provide clues, do not provide a method of distinguishing artists as a class of people from all others.

One very large aspect of artistic action has, however, been left out in the discussion above; that is, the artist's intention. This topic stands out in critical literature and hence deserves separate discussion.

iv. Artistic Intentions

It is often assumed that we must know what an artist intended to do if we are to interpret and evaluate his or her work. As we saw in the last section, historians often point to a particular problem that an artist was trying to solve. Kenneth Clark, for example, tells us that Velázquez intended to "tell the truth about what he saw." To some extent this was a technical problem, but he also provides us with information about Velázquez's individual goals:

> To paint a whole group in such a way that no one seems too prominent, each is easily related to the other, and all breathe the same air: that requires a most unusual gift.[43]

An appreciation of Velázquez's genius requires an understanding of the nature of this problem, the artist's intention to solve it, and his choice of methods for fulfilling the intention.

Thus critics often provide us with details concerning the ways in which artists proceed with their work. They may give us information about changes artists make in their works in order to enhance our appreciation of them—to make us recognize just how apt a particular word or phrase in a poem is, for example. Like many poets, A. E. Housman was a reviser and rereviser of his poems. Realizing that a turn of phrase is "good" often waits upon the realization that it is "better" than alternatives:

> The second line of "Eight O'Clock" is *Sprinkle the quarters on the morning town*. *Sprinkle*, with its little echoes of the rising and falling notes, seems exactly right, as it is; it was so written in all three of the notebook drafts of *Last Poems 15*. But line four has a different history. It now reads *It tossed them down*. The softer *tossed* seems quite inevitable, but Housman did not find it until he had tested and rejected all of the too-noisy or off-tune *dropped, cast, flung, told, dealt, loosed, spilt,* and *pitched*.[44]

Few readers will fully appreciate the presence of 'tossed' unless they are made aware of its superiority to, say, 'flung'. Until one perceives poems as the end products of such trial and error activity, much of the nature of poetry (and more generally art) remains beyond one's grasp.

In other cases the problem is more general, in the sense that each art form of a certain type requires the fulfilling of certain conditions: getting the right number of syllables for a haiku, or the right number of lines for a sonnet, for instance. If readers do not know that a poet intended to write a haiku or a sonnet, much of the nature of the work will be lost on them.

Sometimes critics, historians, and theorists talk more generally about the connection between problems to be solved and art in general, or between aims and styles, and it is clear that intentional activity of a certain kind must be involved. Consider, as an example, this discussion of such broader artistic matters:

> [T]he spatial orientation of units in a work is determined by a number of different influences. The artist must see to it not only that the desired effect prevails but also that the strength of these influences is clearly proportioned in such a way as to make them overrule each other hierarchically or to compensate each other rather than produce a confusing crossfire.[45]

And note Sandler's comment on the development of a whole school of artists:

> The recollections of artists, corroborated by other available documents, including formal statements, public letters, records of meetings, symposia, and lectures, reveal their artistic intentions. Knowledge of the aims and beliefs of the Abstract Expressionists is of prime importance, for it illuminates the actual evolution of their styles.[46]

The latter comment is found on the very first page of Sandler's book, and demonstrates the extent to which critics give a primary place to considerations of artistic intention.

Using the notion of intention, then, our first orange crate could be said to be a work of art and the second not, because it was placed on the grassy space for different reasons. It might be argued that a thing is a work of art only if it is meant to be looked at aesthetically. Minimally, one might insist that the orange crate or moose call be made with the intention of creating a work of art if it is to qualify as such a work. Interpreting 'making a work of art' broadly, I have myself argued elsewhere in support of such a stand.[47] A related position is held by Adrian Stokes in *The Quattro Cento:*

> Art is the symbol of all expression, of the turning of subject into object. The powers of artistic creation gained the deepest reverence of Quattro Cento heroes, not as a symbol of culture so much as a symbol of life. . . . All art has close relation to the life it mirrors, but at no other time could the emblematic significance of art be so personal, so individual, so particular. For the act of artistic creation was itself the specific symbol of release that men were feeling or desiring. Quattro Cento art, so to speak, is art twice over.[48]

If the essential nature of art is its emblematic expression, then what is important is not just seeing a face in a stone but seeing a face put in the stone by a sculptor. Analogously, it would be as emblem that orange crate A and the non–moose made moose call achieve artistic status.

The intentionalist debate has been at the center of theory and criticism for many years. In his *Figures of Speech or Figures of Thought*,[49] Ananda Coomaraswamy argues that we cannot say that something is well done if we do not know what the doer intended. On the other side of the argument, W. K. Wimsatt and Monroe Beardsley admit that the design or plan in an artist's mind may be a cause of what is produced. But, they insist, admitting it as a cause does not admit it as a standard of evaluation; reference to extrinsic information can destroy the reading of a poem. They discuss a quatrain by John Donne as an example:

> Moving of th'earth brings harmes and feare,
>   Men reckon what it did and meant,
> But trepidation of the spheares,
>   Though greater farre, is innocent.

At least one critic has put a great deal of emphasis on Donne's knowledge of the old and new astronomy. Wimsatt and Beardsley respond:

> Perhaps a knowledge of Donne's interest in the new science may add another shade of meaning, an overtone to the stanza in question, though to say even this runs against the words. To make the geocentric and heliocentric antithesis the core of the metaphor is to disregard the English language, to prefer private evidence to public, external to internal.[50]

But what if Donne said somewhere that he intended such a metaphoric core? Wimsatt and Beardsley say earlier in the essay that

> the use of biographical evidence need not involve intentionalism, because while it may be evidence of what the author intended, it may also be evidence of the meaning of his words and the dramatic character of his utterance.[51]

In light of this it would seem that Donne's hypothetical statement—that he intended such a metaphoric core—would constitute evidence that one could use without being dubbed intentionalistic. But would one still be "going against the words"? This is exactly the kind of question which needs answering, and Wimsatt and Beardsley apparently overlook it.

Nevertheless, our problem here does not concern whether or not artistic intentions are relevant to discussions and evaluations of works of art once they have been identified as such. Intentions can only be of use to us if they

somehow distinguish art from nonart. Wimsatt comes a bit closer to this topic
in another essay, "History and Criticism," where he discusses the difference
between poetry and practical messages:

> I take poetry and the practical message to be polar extremes. . . . In
> between one would put, for example, history. . . . and somewhat closer to
> poetry one would put philosophy and science. . . . [They] occupy a position
> of extreme exposure to criticism which proceeds from our own experience.
> It is not, however, the position of maximum exposure. That distinction is
> reserved for poetry—a type of discourse which has traditionally submitted
> to criticism not only of its contentual meaning (in all the referential and
> emotive senses) but of its meaning at those other levels which we call its
> form and style. . . . A fault of style in a scientist is not a scientific fault—
> but in a poet it is a poetic fault.[52]

The continuum that Wimsatt sets up, with practical messages at one end and
poetry at the other, is based on the degree to which the success of the
linguistic entity depends upon its reader having a knowledge of the intention
with which it was produced. Wimsatt here introduces the notion of exposure to
criticism, one which I shall make use of myself in a later chapter. Certainly,
practical messages are not the sort of thing we ordinarily think of as being
open to criticism. Yet such comments as "You didn't make yourself clear," or
"Why didn't you say what you meant?" are common. We even occasionally
criticize style with respect to practical messages: "That was straight to the
point." Clearly, more than exposure to criticism is needed for distinguishing
poems from nonpoems.

The activity involved in the production of works of art is usually such that
most people would classify it as "intentional activity." Some of an artist's
intentions will have to do with the formal properties of a work—choosing
words of a certain length, colors of a certain shade, and so on. Others will
concern nonformal properties, making money, for instance, or praising God.
Some of these latter intentions may at first seem irrelevant to discussions of
artistic objects. Yet time and again our reactions to particular works are
influenced by learning that such intentions were present.

Consider the following first two lines from a poem by Vachel Lindsay:

> Sleep softly . . . eagle forgotten . . . under the stones.
> Time has its way with you there, and the clay has its own.[53]

It makes a great deal of difference for the way one decides to interpret these
lines if one knows that Lindsay intended to eulogize John Altgeld—and not
some poor dead eagle he came across on his way home one evening. Or

suppose I learn that Tennyson was having an affair with a woman who preferred crannied walls to formal gardens. This might substantially alter the
interpretation which I set forth in my discussion of the meaning of "Flower in
the Crannied Wall."

We must, however, be very careful here. Knowing simply that an artist had
a particular intention is not, by itself, enough to insure that that intention is
relevant to the interpretation or evaluation of a given work. Simply knowing
that Tennyson loved a woman who preferred crannied walls to formal gardens
does not mean that when he wrote "Flower in the Crannied Wall" he intended
only to please her, not to convey the idea of a barren and difficult environment. The evidence a reader has for the belief that a particular intention is
connected to a particular interpretation will vary both in type and amount from
work to work. In some instances knowing that a writer had a lover who liked
crannied walls might constitute good reason for believing that the writer made
use of them in a poem simply to please her. But usually much more evidence
will be needed to support such a belief. Further, people perform a great many
actions *intentionally* without being able to state the particular *intention with
which* the act was performed. This is undoubtedly true in the creation of works
of art. It is *particular* intentions of artists which, when we can discover them,
often affect our interpretations.

There are a great many practical and theoretical problems attached to the
use of intentions to explain works of art. Even if we agree that such use is
legitimate, there are problems of access. How do we know what an artist's
intentions were? What if artists themselves are unsure about this? Of the
multiple intentions an artist does have (and which they and we are aware of),
which are relevant? Dickens, for example, intended to effect social changes,
get published, keep his audience involved in his serial tales, and pay bills.
How are we to know when a biographical fact about particular intentions is
relevant?

Even if these questions could be answered, it does not follow that artistic
intentions provide us with a means of distinguishing art from nonart.

Only if a particular intention were discovered which is always and only
present in the creation of works of art would we have a way of distinguishing
art from nonart; classifying an activity as "intentional" does not separate it
from most human activity. Obviously none of the intentions mentioned above
will work. Intending to use a particular color is not restricted to artists any
more than intending to make money is. It may help me to understand Gerard
Manley Hopkins's poetry to know that he was deeply religious and hence must
have had certain intentions when he wrote. But that knowledge alone will not
allow me to conclude that what he wrote must be works of art.

Yet there does seem to be one intention shared by all artists, namely the intention to create a work of art. Will this provide us with a way of distinguishing art from nonart? In the *Critique of Judgment*, Immanuel Kant insists that the intention to create is necessary if an object is to be a work of art:

> By right we ought only to describe art, production through freedom, i.e., through a will that places reason at the basis of its action. For although we like to call the product of bees (regularly built cells of wax) a work of art, this is only by way of analogy; as soon as we feel that this work of theirs is based on no proper rational deliberation, we say that it is a product of nature (or instinct) and as art only ascribe it to their Creator.

> If as sometimes happens, in searching through a bog we come upon a bit of shaped wood, we do not say, that is a product of nature, but of art. Its producing cause has conceived a purpose to which the plank owes its form—But if we call anything absolutely a work of art, in order to distinguish it from a natural effect, we always understand by that a work of man. [54]

Kant is maintaining that a work of art must be the product of conscious, rational, deliberate thought. It is this which distinguishes it from a natural object. John Dewey takes a similar line:

> Suppose for the sake of illustration that a finely wrought object, one whose texture and proportions are highly pleasing in perception, has been believed to be a product of some primitive people. Then there is discovered evidence that proves it to be an accidental natural product. As an external thing, it is now precisely what it was before. Yet at once it ceases to be a work of art, and becomes a natural "curiosity." It now belongs in a museum of natural history, not in a museum of art. [55]

The extent to which I agree with Kant and Dewey will become apparent in the next chapter. However, there are problems with insisting that an object cannot be called a work of art unless we know that it was made with that intention. Suppose the creator is not available? Or suppose he or she lies or is self-deceived?

And even if we admit its necessity, the intention to create a work of art must also be a *sufficient* condition if we are to have our test for differentiating art from nonart. If it were a sufficient condition, then all anyone would have to do to create a work of art would be to have that intention while making something. Perhaps this smacks too much of "black magic" to be acceptable to most of us. If only the proper intention were needed, how could one ever fail, assuming the presence of the intention to create, to produce a work of art? When failure becomes impossible, is there any sense left in success? Until these questions are answered, we are forced to look elsewhere for the defining characteristic of works of art.

v. The Content of a Work of Art

I believe that the greatest amount of space in discussions of art works has been devoted to what is usually called the *content* or *subject matter* of those works. Questions raised in this connection take a variety of forms: what it is about, what is being said, what the idea behind all of it is, what is being portrayed, or described, or represented, or expressed. The answers to these questions range from the very simple to the very complex, and critics often disagree in their answers.

In addition to dealing with questions about the particular content of individual works, some writers are concerned with broader issues related to content. For example, Longinus and Ruskin believed that content plays an essential theoretical role in being, ultimately, the thing that distinguishes great art from lesser art. This position might lead one to hope that content could provide a means of distinguishing art from nonart as well.

Both of these aspects of criticism, interpreting the content of specific art works and basing a theory about the nature of art on differences in content, will play a significant role in the theory I present in this chapter and the next. Thus we must look at examples of both sorts of critical concerns.

The use of symbol systems in all of the arts has provided a more or less metaphoric way of talking about the necessity of *reading* a work. That we cannot have access to literature written in a language we do not know is obvious. Even literature written in our own tongue is often obscure and beyond our immediate comprehension. The same is true with the other arts. Compare the Daumier and Ohman cartoons in figures 8 and 9, for example. Although both deal ostensibly with "balance," they must be interpreted in radically different ways. And the fact that the content of the latter is so much more readily accessible to us depends upon the mutual knowledge we share with the contemporary cartoonist, something we lack in the case of the Daumier cartoon. One way of thinking about criticism and history, then, is as helping viewers to overcome such difficulties in interpretation, to learn to "read the language" in which a particular sonata or painting—as well as poem—is written.

There is no way of providing examples of all sorts of the things that critics talk about which fall under the general heading of "subject matter." But I have chosen a few which I myself have found interesting and which exemplify the

Fig. 8. Honoré Daumier, *European Equilibrium*. Courtesy of Fogg Art Museum, Harvard University, Cambridge, Massachusetts.

Fig. 9. Jack Ohman, *There, It's Balanced.*

way in which critics bring us to perceive things which we would have missed on our own, either because we are ignorant of some relevant fact or because our eyes or ears are not sufficiently sharp or well trained.

I said above that some descriptions of a work's content are very simple: "There's a woman in a red hat"; "It's about harvesting corn." At times it may seem that such comments are superfluous; critics often point out things that, we may think, anyone with normal senses and intelligence should have perceived unassisted. Consider Richard Benedict's remarks on the honeycomb molding in the Alhambra as a case in point:

> This honeycomb of stalactitic mouldings in the Alhambra Palace forms part of the base of a cupola which in turn supports a fantastic vault of the same stalactites (mukkarnas). By breaking up the surface of the ceiling in this way the Moorish workers were able to achieve an effect of insubstantiality, an effect also aimed at on the intricately patterned walls and the openwork of the arches in the court arcades.[56]

Obviously anyone who has never seen the Alhambra Palace or pictures of it will learn something from Benedict's comments. But does someone actually visiting the Alhambra get anything from them? Won't every visitor see the honeycomb arches and notice the "insubstantiality" thus created? (See plate IV.) I think we must answer, "No." Tourists often miss the most obvious features of such landmarks if left completely on their own. Even the most sophisticated visitors purchase guidebooks in order to be sure to look for what is there. After reading such passages as Benedict's, we can hardly fail to look at the stalactites and at the way in which they are related in an open grillwork; we look also for the "insubstantiality" created thereby. We may further compare it mentally to a heavy barrel vault, or directly to the Gate of Justice in the same complex.

Notice that in his description Benedict tells us not only what is contained in the structure (the stalactites), but also points to the created effect (insubstantiality). This is a very common combination. Critics provide us with a description of the formal and/or representative features of a work and then explain to us what the expressive result of these features is:

> Called "hybrids" by Breton, Gorky's visceral amalgams of natural phenomena constituted imaginary landscapes that are also tabletops, echoing his earlier Cubist still lifes. By integrating motifs from diverse sources, Gorky followed the Surrealist practice of "putting nature out of place" to suggest irrational and startling juxtapositions. Indeed, his desire for this kind of cryptic lyricism led him to use ambiguous motifs that lend themselves to multiple connotations and to immerse them in an atmosphere that invites reverie. Central to Gorky's poetry, as to Surrealism in general was the drama of sex, which was projected in the interaction of erotic signs: softly rounded and yielding shapes and pudenda-like crevices that evoke a warm, tender voluptuousness, and hard, bony thorn-and-claw-like protuberances that suggest hostile, even cruel phallic aggressions.[57] (See figure 10)

Sandler here does not simply tell us what is there to be seen, as if he were trying to get someone who could only see the duck also to see the rabbit. By referring to things not in the picture, namely surrealist and cubist practices in general, we find out something more about the content of what we are looking at, something that relates the content here to the content of other works.

Critics and historians typically describe the content of works in ways that lead us to other works, other artists, or conditions in which the work was created. In literary criticism we are often given incidents from a story augmented by references to things outside the story and then shown how they relate to a more general theme, idea, or feeling which the work as a whole expresses. Thus in Leavis's discussion of *Daniel Deronda* we find this:

> It is, of course, possible to imagine a beautiful, clever and vital girl, with "That sense of superior claims which made a large part of her conscious-

Pl. I. Theodore Géricault, *The Raft of the Medusa.* Louvre, Cliché Musées Nationaux Paris.

Pl. II. Battersea Park, fall, 1977. Author's photo.

Pl. III. El Greco, *View of Toledo*. Metropolitan Museum of Art, New York, Mrs. H. O. Havemeyer, 1929, The H. O. Havemeyer Collection.

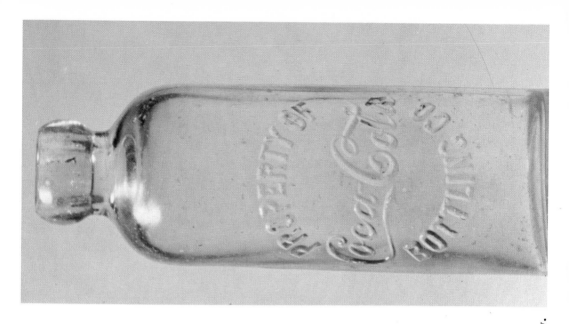

Pl. V. Early Coke Bottle. Courtesy, Archives, The Coca-Cola Company.

Pl. IV. Court of the Lions, The Alhambra. Dennis Eaton photo.

Pl. VII. Birdbath. Author's photo.

Pl. VI. Souvenir Wallhanging. University of Minnesota Photo Lab.

Fig. 10. Arshile Gorky, *The Liver Is the Cock's Comb*. Albright-Knox Art Gallery, Buffalo, New York, gift of Seymour H. Knox.

ness" (George Eliot's phrase for Gwendolen, but it applies equally to Isabel), whose egoism yet shouldn't be as much open to the criticism of an intelligent woman as Gwendolen's. But it is hard to believe that, in life, she could be as free from qualities inviting a critical response as the Isabel Archer seen by James. Asking of Gwendolen, why, though a mere girl, she should be everywhere a centre of deferential attention, George Eliot says (Chapter IV): "The answer may seem to lie quite on the surface: —in her beauty, a certain unusualness about her, a decision of will which made itself felt in her graceful movements and clear unhesitating tones, so that if she came into the room on a rainy day when everybody else was flaccid and the use of things in general was not apparent to them, there seemed to be a sudden reason for keeping up the forms of life." James might very well have been glad to have found these phrases for his heroine. But George Eliot isn't satisfied with the answer: she not only goes on, as James would hardly have done, to talk about the girl's "inborn energy of egoistic desire," she is very specific and concrete in exhibiting the play of that energy—the ways in which it imposes her claims on the people around her. And it is not enough to reply that James doesn't need to be specific to this effect—even granting, as we may, that the two authors are dealing with different girls: it is so plain that George Eliot knows more about hers than he about his, and that this accounts for an important part of the ostensible difference. [58]

Here we find Leavis comparing two heroines created by different authors. I said earlier in this chapter that comparison is a basic tool of criticism. Comparing and contrasting contents is as frequent in discussions of the content of works as it is in discussion of artists. Not only do such comparisons further our understanding of many works; they also provide a means of evaluation:

> Fanny Burney's fiction is filled with figures who remind us of Colonel Brandon or Willoughby or Mrs. Bennet, and although one can argue that these were common types, the details of their treatment in Jane Austen's early work are often reminiscent of Fanny Burney. More significantly, the struggle between personal affection and family pride in Cecilia may have suggested the major themes of *Pride and Prejudice*; certainly the title was taken from the conclusion to *Cecilia*, where Dr. Lyster points the story's moral. "The whole of this unfortunate business . . . has been the result of Pride and Prejudice. . . . Yet this, however, remember: if to Pride and Prejudice you owe your miseries, so wonderfully is the good and evil balanced, that to Pride and Prejudice you will also owe their termination." But these similarities between *Pride and Prejudice* and Fanny Burney's novels only intensify our sense of Jane Austen's achievement in transforming the conventions of "the land of fiction." [59]

Nor is discussion of content limited to the obviously subject matter–laden literature and representational art. Music is also often discussed in terms of what it says, expresses, or describes. In his book *The Language of Music*, Deryck Cooke argues that the elements of music, pitch, intervallic tension, volume, and tempo act as a vocabulary through which a wide range of human emotions can be expressed:

> To fall from the tonic to the dominant, taking in the optimistic major seventh and sixth, is to express an incoming emotion of joy, an acceptance or welcoming of comfort, consolation, or fulfillment. The term is clearly a near-synonym of the major 5–4–3–2–1, with which it often combines into a descending major scale, in the way that the ascending triadic figures 1–3–5 and 5–1–3 combine and intermingle. However, when it is used separately, the fact that it ends on the dominant gives it a more open, continuing feeling towards the future, compared with 5–3–1, which suggests finality. [60]

Cooke cites examples of the use of this expression in Dunstable's *Veni sancte spiritus*, Bach's *St. Matthew Passion*, Mozart's *Mass in C Minor*, and Verdi's *La Traviata*; and says,

. . . it acts firmly as the ground bass for the final duet of Monteverdi's *L'Incoronazione di Poppea,* in which Nero and Poppea, all their worries over, welcome the opportunity to enjoy their love; majestically, in the Sanctus in Bach's B Minor Mass; and actively again, in the angel's chorus "Glory to God" in Handel's *Messiah* (the fulfillment of the long-awaited "good tidings of great joy.")[61]

Critics and historians also frequently uncover and/or explain the symbolism of artistic works. Indeed, digging and hunting for hidden symbols consumes a major part of many critics' and historians' time. And convincing an audience that a symbol is present in a work almost invariably necessitates reference to facts or traditions not present in the works themselves. Desmond Collins elucidates cave paintings by telling us,

The paintings at El Castello are again predominantly of animals, but there are also hand silhouettes made on walls, and many of the strange oblong signs known as tectiforms, which are brightly coloured and formed with lines and dots. The importance of the hand in primitive symbolism is known in other early cultures such as that of Egypt, while the tectiforms have been variously interpreted as buildings, traps, and sex symbols.[62]

And Kenneth Clark explains:

The group in the right hand boat [in Raphael's cartoon "The Miraculous Draught of Fishes"] represents art for art's sake. During the first twenty years of the sixteenth century, a foreshortened nude figure and, in particular, a foreshortened shoulder were thought to be the most gratifying form on which the eye could rest, and in the two sons of Zebedee bending over their nets, Raphael is consciously giving a proof of his mastery of *disegno*, the key word of the Renaissance which meant drawing, design, and formal convention all in one.[63]

In these two examples, we are given information about the use of symbols in periods from which we are removed and hence of which we may be ignorant. By pointing out the value to the Renaissance of a foreshortened shoulder, the modern viewers are bound to look at the shoulder in Raphael's cartoon as they come to recognize its symbolic importance.

Critics especially delight in providing us with their insights into more obscure references. Critics who specialize in "difficult" writers such as Joyce or Nabokov, are particularly adept at this. Few and far between are the readers of *Pale Fire,* for example, who can detect on their own the plays on words which Mary McCarthy explains in her review of that novel.[64] Likewise, Andrew Field, in his discussion of the same novel, quotes the Samuel Johnson epigram about shooting cats and tells us,

The epigram in fact makes sense only when it is seen as a statement by
Nabokov about the novel, or a statement by Shade about Kinbote. . . . The
reader who is willing to march through Boswell's biography in search of it
will find (on page 1,038 of the Modern Library edition) that the remark
about the cat Hodge occurs on the same page as a remark by Boswell that a
work was to be written by Johnson on the Boswell family, based on papers to
be furnished by Boswell. This plan, Boswell informs us, was soon put aside
in favor of other projects, which strongly suggests that the epigraph does
indeed have something to say about *Pale Fire* as a whole, should it be
thought that the epigraph is simply a whimsical bit of nonsense signifying
nothing about the novel.[65]

I, for one, am quite unwilling to march through Boswell, but I'm glad Field did
it for me.

The dispute with respect to the application of psychoanalytic theory to
literature rears its head again with respect to the explanation of the contents of
art works. Ernest Jones, as we have seen, is one of the foremost proponents of
interpreting details of works according to Freudian analysis. Thus he points to
details which might be overlooked by readers of *Hamlet*, say to the fact that
Claudius spreads the tale that his brother was stung by a serpent in an
orchard—symbolizing the woman in whose arms the king was murdered.[66]
And, he claims to explain in this fashion things that have long puzzled other
critics.

On the pedestal of (the Madonna of Zanobi Bracci) . . . are several harpies,
which are, of course, entirely out of place in a subject of this character. . . .
Critics have been completely mystified by this, but, if my suggestion concerning Andrea's unconscious attitude towards his wife is correct it should
not be difficult of explanation.[67]

Others, of course, are as unwilling to accept psychoanalytic explanations of
a work's content as they are to accept psychoanalytic explanations of its
creation. Gombrich cites a story told by Sabartés about Picasso's relationship
with his father, and warns us that not all of the psychological explanation he
might refer to actually illuminates for us the original object:

[Does] this private meaning really glow in the work before you? Could you
surmise it from this poster (Dove) if Sabartés had not obliged us acciden-
tally with this telling episode? Frankly I doubt it. Though the pigeon must
be charged and overcharged with memories and meanings for Picasso,
though he cannot but have enjoyed this opportunity of doing a pigeon, as his
father did, but one that would fly over half the world, I see no evidence that
this private meaning reverberates in the particular work, that it is com-
municated.[68]

But the really great critics and historians such as Gombrich and Leavis manage to retell or redescribe for us the contents even of works with which we are already familiar, in ways which further illuminate these works for us, and in ways which provide nearly as much pleasure as do the works themselves. I believe that this fact implies much concerning the way in which art and nonart differ and shall return to it in the final chapter, where we shall see that the various critical tactics we have considered here with respect to content will be related to the general nature of art. But a description of a work's content does not serve as a guarantee that it is (or is not) a work of art. "It discusses gamekeeping" is equally true of articles in *Field and Stream* and *Lady Chatterley's Lover*. Pigeons, unconscious attitudes toward wives, hands, and the fulfillment of joy are also the sorts of things that can be dealt with both artistically and nonartistically.

But can more general observations be made about the content of works of art that will provide a basis for the distinction we are seeking? Longinus asserted that great art is lofty, that it presents subjects that elevate our mind.[69] John Ruskin insisted that great art must have noble, and thus ennobling, subject matter.[70] This is a theme of many of Ruskin's works. However, Longinus and Ruskin to the contrary, there is no significant way of delineating the subject matter which differentiates art from nonart. It may even be true that all great art is "lofty" or "noble," but unfortunately these terms tell us much too little. Attempts to define 'art' in terms of content are either too broad or too narrow. One attempt at defining art in terms of subject matter, which illustrates problems typical of such attempts, is that of Tolstoy in *What Is Art?*[71] There he defines art as the transmission via media such as sounds, colors, or words, of feelings and, in particular for modern society, the transmission of feelings that will promote universal brotherhood. Essentially what he insists is that the content of art be *moral*.[72] I once asked a class to go to an exhibit at a university gallery and, on the basis of Tolstoy's definition, determine if there were any works of art on display. Their reactions emphasized the weaknesses of the definition. What are "feelings of brotherhood"? How does one know when they are evoked? Can't "immoral content" such as prostitutes or drunkards do more to arouse our sympathy for fellow beings than "moral content" such as nuns and reformers?

But even if the questions concerning the meaning of morality could be settled, Tolstoy's definition still does not solve our problem. Any definition of 'work of art' in terms of subject matter, even if we include as a necessary condition the use of media such as words or colors, is bound to suffer from a fatal flaw. If the representation of certain things rather than others, or the expression of certain beliefs rather than others is to serve as a way of distinguishing art from nonart, it must be the case that art and only art can represent these. That is, even if having a particular kind of content or subject matter were a necessary condition of a thing's being a work of art (as it seems to be for Tolstoy), it would not be sufficient unless art alone had such content. This is, of course, absurd, If the belief expressed in a work of art made that thing a work of art, then the mere statement of the belief expressed in a work of art would itself be a work of art. And if the subject matter of a work of art also became the subject matter of non–works of art such as political posters or newspaper articles, then the work would lose its status. Hence the distinction must be sought elsewhere.

vi. The Function of a Work of Art

Another basic category of interest in art is pragmatic, that is, people have been and continue to be interested in the purposes to which art is put and in its effects. As Harold Osborne notes, "Since through the greater part of human history the so-called fine arts were regarded as handicrafts among others, not distinguished as a class, and since art objects like other products of human industry were designed to serve a purpose recognised and approved by the society in which they arose, this practical interest in the purpose of the arts is the most general and in a sense the most natural of all."[73] Instrumental or functional theories of art have been identified by aestheticians as one of the basic categories of such theories.[74] Plato, disgusted by the fact that most artists did not fulfill the function of providing Truth, dismissed them from the Republic; Aristotle, insisting that the arts, like everything else, can be understood only when their purposes are known, defined tragedy as aiming at a special kind of pleasure.

But the vagueness of the term 'function' is evident in the preceding paragraph. There are tremendous differences in thinking of art as producing objects of "practical interest" as opposed to meeting human needs for pleasure or as fulfilling the abstract function Plato envisioned.

The more narrow sense of 'function' is used when we are told, for instance, that a particular column is weight-bearing and thus must be of a certain size. Guido Ballo insists that one *must* recognize such practical functions of a work of art—a piece of architectural sculpture, for example—before it can be correctly perceived. There is a significant difference between functional decoration such as the capitals and columns of Greek temples, he says, and superimposed decoration:

Fig. 11. Arc de Triomphe d'Etoile. Photo © Arch. Phot., Paris/ SPADEM-/VAGA, New York.

When we turn to the Arc de Triomphe in the Place de l-Etoile, Paris, we find a work which in itself is anything but beautiful and reminds us of stage scenery. Nevertheless, it vindicates itself because it is part of the urban scene and because its decorative effect is essentially due to the fact that it is the meeting-point of a number of city streets. This enables it to assume a different aspect and to give vitality to its setting and harmony to its surroundings.[75] (See figure 11).

This narrower sense of *function* also operates when critics and historians point to the consequences of particular works as, for example, when we are told that Dickens's works were influential in social reform that took place in England in the nineteenth century. Thus Annette Rubenstein quotes from a letter which Dickens wrote:

I went some weeks ago to Manchester, and saw the *worst* cotton mill. And then I saw the *best*. *Ex uno disce omnes*. There was no great difference between them. . . . So far as seeing goes, I have seen enough for my purposes, and what I have seen has disgusted and astonished me beyond all measure. I mean to strike the heaviest blow in my power for these unfortunate creatures, but whether I shall do so in Nickleby or wait some other opportunity, I have not yet determined.[76]

In addition to pointing to consequences which individual artists' hope to bring about, critics and historians often describe schools or movements in terms of common goals or interests. Irving Sandler, for one, discusses the sociopolitical goal shared by a group of artists and their supporters (or critics) in our own century:

> Given the artists' social consciousness, it was natural for them to respond to calls for social action. . . . The Communists pressured artists not only to devote full time and energy to politics, but also to adopt a Social Realist position. . . . To the Communist Party art was a weapon in the class struggle, subservient to politics. The function was propagandistic, to incite the masses to revolution. Its subject matter had to be what proletarian novelist Mike Gold termed "the suffering of the hungry, persecuted and heroic millions," and its form an easily understood figuration. To convey its message as forcibly as possible, art had to be executed in an aggressive declamatory manner, painted on a large scale, and placed where it could be widely seen—all factors that favored the use of mural paintings in public sites.[77]

We must, however, remember that, as interesting and useful as such explanations are, there is a fundamental difference between the function, purposes, or social consequences associated with individual works or groups of artists and the function of art as such. We may use knowledge about what consequences an artist intended his work to produce in order to interpret it; but it in no way follows that all works have such consequences. Someone may make a pair of scissors to use to kill a spouse—and knowing that may explain certain features of those scissors to us. Yet it certainly does not follow that the function of scissors generally is to murder people. Nor will the phrase "something to cut with" allow us to distinguish scissors from nonscissors. Nor, it should be noticed, will knowing the general function of scissors necessarily do much to help us understand the particular pair of scissors manufactured with murderous intent. We cannot deny that some works of art have been used—and have been intended to be used—to stir up political emotions. But it would be nonsense to conclude that this is either the primary or sole function of art. Conversely Horace's *dulce et utile*, for example, won't go very far toward explaining particular works to us.

But there are theorists who do more than provide information concerning the function of a particular work, who believe that there is a function which art in general has. Art has been viewed, for example, as functioning primarily to improve the moral character of its audience. I believe that such theories are connected to a basic attitude toward aesthetic value. We can all agree that art is valuable, very valuable. Some theorists appear to believe that goodness (and hence value) is, first and foremost, moral goodness. Thus the aesthetic value of an object or event is ultimately seen to derive from its moral value. How, they seem to ask, could art be valuable if it didn't *do* something useful above and beyond merely being pleasant? Thus I. A. Richards begins one essay, "The value of the experiences which we seek from the arts does not lie . . . in the exquisiteness of the moment of consciousness; a set of isolated ecstasies is not a sufficient explanation."[78] With this assumption in mind, he later defines poetry (and simultaneously distinguishes it from science) in terms of the function it has: organizing and arousing impulses and attitudes (rather than beliefs, which is the function of science). Thus Richards's theory of poetry is fundamentally pragmatic.

As we saw in section iv of this chapter, Tolstoy insists that art must have a moral content. This follows directly upon his definition of art, a definition which exemplifies another function often identified by theorists as a defining feature of 'art'. (In Tolstoy the moral and expressive functions are bound together, but they need not be.) Tolstoy says:

> To evoke in oneself a feeling one has once experienced, and having evoked it in oneself, then, by means of movements, lines, colors, sounds, or forms expressed in words, so to transmit that feeling that others may experience the same feeling—that is the activity of art. . . .
>
> Art is a human activity consisting in this, that one man consciously, by means of certain external signs, hands on to others feelings he has lived through, and that other people are infected by these feelings and also experience them.[79]

The function of art, then, is the transmission or expression of feelings. It is a way of uniting the artist and the audience to such a degree that the viewer, reader, or listener begins to feel that the work is his or her own.

Of course, not everyone has agreed that all works of art have a special, not to say the same, function. Indeed, the very lack of any function at all has been what some have insisted distinguishes art from other things. As we saw in chapter 1, several theorists, beginning with Edmund Burke, have located the uniqueness of art in the disinterested attitude which accompanies the production and enjoyment of aesthetic objects generally and works of art specifically.

Function can be helpful to us only if we can give an affirmative answer to the question: Do art objects have a function which nonart objects do not have? We can answer this question only after the following one has been settled: Does art have a function? Kant's "purposiveless purpose" which, it seems to me, attempts to have it both ways at once, is a famous case of the difficulty encountered when one tries to answer this second, more basic, question. In order to skirt these problems, let us agree with Richards and Tolstoy that art does have a function. Even granting that, we find ourselves unable to distinguish art from nonart on this basis.

As a case study, let us consider Tolstoy's suggestion that the function of art is the transmission of feelings. Expression theories are among the most firmly entrenched in the history of aesthetics; versions of them are as numerous as their advocates. In its strongest form 'art' is defined as "artifacts [collections of sounds, words, colors, and so on] that express feelings." 'Express' has been interpreted in many ways, but these interpretations can roughly be classified as belonging to one of the following:

1. 'x expresses y' if and only if the artist was y when he/she produced x. (A poem expresses sadness if and only if the artist was sad when he/she wrote it.)

2. 'x expresses y' if and only if x's audience feels y when perceiving x. (A song expresses sadness if and only if its hearers are made to feel sad by it.)

3. 'x expresses y' if and only if x has some of the properties that y people have. (A painting expresses sadness if and only if it has some of the properties that sad people have, e.g., *droopy* lines, *somber* colors.)

Tolstoy's theory clearly combines (1) and (2); for he insisted that real art both express feelings artists actually have and evoke these feelings in and hence communicate them to members of the audience.

This is a deviation from the standard use of 'express'. Rarely do we deny that someone expressed anger if we are not in fact angered ourselves by the person. Yet Tolstoy demands this in art. There are many people who argue that they think it odd to say, "That's a sad poem, but of course no one who read it has ever been saddened by it." At the same time most of us want to leave room for the possibility that not everyone who reads a sad poem must then become sad.

Expression theories of art inherit many ambiguities which we find in ordinary talk about expression. The theories deserve far more attention than can be given them here. Suffice it to say that no theory yet has satisfactorily dealt with these and a host of related problems. At best, his and other expression theories of art point out *one* function of art, and it is not a defining function. By now the reader must anticipate the remark about to come. The expression of feelings (even if we were clear as to what this entailed) would allow us to distinguish art from nonart only if this were unique to works of art. But feelings are expressed (and transmitted) in many ways other than by artworks—facial expressions, overt actions, letters to the editor, cries.

Nor do we fare any better when we shift from the psychological to the social function of art. In discussing art as a weapon of social change, Edmund Wilson says, "It is true that art may be a weapon, but in the case of some of the greatest works of art, some of those which have the longest carry-over value, it is difficult to see that any important part of this value is due to their functioning as weapons."[80] This is true, I believe, of all these functions. Horace's *dulce et utile* doesn't serve to distinguish art from raspberry-flavored penicillin. Wellek and Warren are right when they say that the function of literature is to produce the pleasures that accompany nonacquisitive contemplation; but that doesn't separate art from nonart either. Nor is it any help to say, as they do, that ". . .poetry has many possible functions. Its prime and chief function is fidelity to its own nature."[81] For ultimately, as Rader and Jessup comment, that is the function of everything.

> There is nothing so special about art as the purists suppose. Intrinsic attention to qualities, with the "aesthetic emotion" that accompanies it, is not peculiar to art or to rare aesthetic experiences—it is an everyday occurrence in our perception of nature and the human environment. . . . The purists who would fence art off from life cut the ground out from under their own feet—because the enjoyment of intrinsic perception and interest in form, which they point to as peculiar to art appreciation, are among the most common and elementary of all life interests. When we say that art is the creation of aesthetic value, therefore, we do not mean that there is an elusive emotion or an exclusive qualitative essence which art and art alone exhibits. Art creates aesthetic value, not by hermetic isolation from life, but by making life values fascinating to contemplate.[82]

If the function of art is identical to the function of other things (and facial expressions as well as poems communicate feelings and organize and arouse emotions and attitudes), and if art appreciation is a common rather than unique experience, then function cannot be the basis of the distinction between art and those other things.

vii. The Setting of a Work of Art

A further attempt at distinguishing art objects might be based upon the belief that works of art are necessarily the result of cultural conditions. Thus, it might be claimed that in the absence of knowledge concerning its cultural or historic context, the question whether or not something is a work of art cannot be settled. This position has appeal for those who believe that what counts as a work of art in one historical period or cultural setting may not count as one in another place and time. Just another spoon to a cook in the twelfth century B.C. may be an art object in the twentieth.

That critics often refer to the cultural milieu of works is both asserted and exemplified in the following passage:

> We take for granted the social and cultural milieu and philosophy that produced Mozart. As western people, the socio-cultural thinking of eighteenth-century Europe comes to us as a historic legacy that is a continuous and organic part of the twentieth-century West. The socio-cultural philosophy of the Negro in America (as a continuous historical phenomenon) is no less specific and no less important for any intelligent critical speculation about the music that came out of it. And again, this is not a plea for narrow sociological analysis of jazz, but rather that this music cannot be completely understood (in critical terms) without some attention to the attitudes which produced it. [83]

One of the greatest difficulties we encounter in attempting to understand art objects arises when we are confronted with artifacts greatly removed from us culturally or temporally. As Brunius explains, "We are ethnocentric in the sense that we act and think and evaluate inside the decorum of our cultures, to the pattern of which the tacitly implied rules of art belong. Changes in decorum depend upon time and cultural milieu, age, temper, education, class." [84] According to Guido Ballo, overcoming this ethnocentricity is absolutely essential, and, fortunately, possible. "A man with critical eyes," he says, "knows how to change his angle of vision so as to be able to view a work of art properly, and provided we know something about these things, he studies the various trends, the historical, cultural, and social conditions of the time when the work was created and in relation to the career of the artist and the civilization he reflects." [85] We must, for example, be aware of the fact that art originally was not separate from religion, magic, ethics, and politics: "If we consider [a Lower Congo] fetish exclusively as a work of art and treat it as we do the works of Breughel, Rembrandt or Masaccio (which are equally expressive, but were produced in different cultural surroundings and form part of more complex civilizations) we are adopting an ambiguous method which the study of history has made superfluous." [86] We combat our ethnocentricity by learning something about the culture in which works are produced. Hence, when critics refer to social or cultural conditions, they try to provide us with the information necessary to our understanding.

Yet it is not only in connection with objects as remote as Lower Congo fetishes that we find references to facts about the culture in which art objects were produced. Sometimes these facts are pointed to in the course of discussing the attitudes or outlook of a particular artist. For example, Berenson's discussion of Titian includes the following:

> The overwhelming triumph of Spain entailed still other consequences. It brought home to all Italians, even to the Venetians, the sense of the individual's helplessness before organized power—a sense which, as we have seen, the early Renaissance, with its belief in the omnipotence of the individual, totally lacked. This was not without a decided influence on art. In the last three decades of his long career, Titian did not paint man as if he were as free from care and as fitted to his environment as a lark on an April morning. Rather did he represent man as acting on his environment and suffering from his reactions.[87]

We also find critics and historians using social and cultural facts to explain formal properties of works. Again from Berenson:

> The growing delight in life with the consequent love of health, beauty, and joy were felt more powerfully in Venice than anywhere else in Italy. The explanation of this may be found in the character of the Venetian government which was such that it gave little room for the satisfaction of the passion for personal glory (which was felt elsewhere in Italy), and kept its citizens so busy in duties of state that they had small leisure for learning. Some of the chief passions of the Renaissance thus finding no outlet in Venice, the other passions insisted all the more on being satisfied. Venice, moreover, was the only state in Italy which was enjoying, and for many generations had been enjoying, internal peace. This gave the Venetians a love of comfort, of ease, and of splendour, a refinement of manner, and humaneness of feeling, which made them the first modern people in Europe. . . . Painting, accommodating itself to the new ideas, found that it could not attain to satisfactory representation merely by form and colour, but that it required light and shadow and effects of space.[88]

Or in order to explain the general content of works of a given period, historians often refer to facts about the society.

> It is important, if we are to understand the nature of the literature of the era, to emphasize how bitterly the Mr. Bounderbys, who played so vital a part in shaping the Victorian world, were opposed to art and how conscientiously they strove to degrade it. From the Utilitarians who preferred push-pin to poetry to the hard-faced men whom Keynes watched negotiating the Treaty of Versailles, the industrial bourgeoisie as a class (one does not forget of course enlightened individuals struggling against the current) hated and feared the implications of any artistic effort of realism and integrity. And throughout the century, from the days of Shelley's Castlereagh through those of Dickens' Gradgrind to the triumph of Matthew Arnold's Philistines,

honest writers were bound to feel a deep revulsion against the underlying principles and the warped relationships of the society they lived in.[89]

The times in which they were created tell us something about art objects. But the converse is true as well. Consider these two passages:

These paintings [in caves in Mediterranean coastal provinces of Spain] provide probably the best insight into the social institutions of any primitive society of the past. One in the Agua Amarga cave in Teruel shows a band of hunters running across the scene, possibly indicating the tribal group. Some of them have feather head-dresses in American Indian style. No clear sign of a chief or nobles is to be detected in any of the group pictures, and accordingly we may visualize the kind of simple tribal organization found among modern hunters such as the Bushmen of the Kalahari desert. In such a tribe the leader would be accorded his position solely by virtue of the respect in which he was held.[90]

The confrontation of Islam and Christianity in medieval Spain was bound to have remarkable consequences. Each side was convinced that it possessed the unique spiritual truth which must be revealed to the unfortunate unbeliever for his own good. This evangelical obligation was the justification for aggression, persecution and mutual suspicion, alternating with long periods of harmony in which Moslems and Christians worked side by side. The profound effects of this link between East and West were long lasting and can be seen even now in the unique character of Spain and in the diversity and quality of Spanish art.[91]

Such comments do not "naturally" belong to history or to art criticism, or to anthropology or to religion; they can be used both to explain the character of the work before us or to enlighten us about the period. And there are those who consider this a great problem. We have earlier encountered the worry that reference to extrinsic information can be distracting, and cultural considerations may, after all, lead one to turn attention away from the work itself to the culture in which it was created. Yet this need not happen. What precedes and follows comments of the kind cited above will indicate the author's main intent. Do we launch into a discussion of primitive political systems or of color and shape? Does the author continue to explain the special character of Spanish art or the special character of Spain? The fact that an author is not primarily an *art* historian does not mean that he or she cannot further our understanding or appreciation of works of art.

Nonetheless, we are confronted with a by now familiar problem. It is not enough that reference to culture sometimes helps us to understand works of art. In order for sociocultural considerations to enable us to distinguish art from nonart, a general theory must be forthcoming. There are three likely places where such a culture-based theory can be sought in the twentieth century: in the area known as sociology of art, in Marxism, and in institutional theories of art.

A theory of the sort we need does not present itself in the first of these. The sociology of art tends to be concerned with art as one institution among many, that is, as exhibiting special patterns of social behavior.[92] Rarely are there discussions of individual art works or genres, and then only when they exemplify larger patterns. Is art a primary or a secondary institution? How does the artist's role in his or her work-institution differ from that of others? How does art compare to other institutions? These are examples of the sorts of questions art sociologists deal with. As Milton Albrecht explains, the art object is to be understood as "an essential link in an extensive network of social and cultural relations."[93]

This attitude toward art is exemplified in Lucien Goldmann's "The Sociology of Literature," where he describes the premises of genetic structural society:

> The categorical structures, which govern the collective consciousness and which are transposed into the imaginary universe created by the artist, are neither conscious nor unconscious in the Freudian sense of the word, which presupposes a repression: they are nonconscious processes which, in certain respects, are akin to those which govern the functioning of the muscular or nervous structures and determine the particular character of our movements and gestures. That is why in most cases, the bringing to light of these structures and, implicitly, the comprehension of the work can be achieved neither by immanent literary study nor by study directed towards the conscious intentions of the writer or towards the psychology of the unconscious, but only by research of the structuralist and sociological type.[94]

It is not my wish to attempt to refute structuralism or to deny that such structures exist. Certainly interesting features of works are pointed out in the course of such discussions. When such structures are discovered, claims Albrecht, ". . . certain details of the text, which had not in any way attracted the research worker's attention up to that point, suddenly appear to be both important and significant."[95] Consider, for example, his discussion of Goethe's *Faust:*

> Faust addressed himself to the Spirits of the Macrocosm and of the Earth, which correspond to the philosophies of Spinoza and Hegel. The reply of the second Spirit sums up the very essence of the play and, even more, of the first part of it—the opposition between, on the one hand, the philosophy

of enlightenment, whose ideal was knowledge and comprehension, and, on the other hand, dialectical philosophy, centered on action. The reply of the Spirit of the Earth—"You resemble the Spirit you understand, and not me"—is not merely a refusal; it is also its justification. Faust is still at the level of "understanding," that is to say at the level of the Spirit of Macrocosm, which is precisely what he wanted to outdistance. He will not be able to meet the Spirit of the Earth until the moment when he finds the true translation of the Gospel according to Saint John ("In the beginning was action") and when he accepts the past with Mephistopheles.[96]

The important thing to notice here is that such thinkers are not interested in determining whether a given object is art or not, but in seeing how these objects, once identified as such, fit into larger social structures. And if I understand the structuralist position correctly, most of its adherents believe that these structures are not only embodied in art but in many other things—political, religious, and economic institutions—as well.

As elsewhere, Marxism has exerted a great deal of influence in twentieth-century aesthetics. Marx and Engels themselves did not insist that art is always or should idealy be political. Like sociologists of art, Marxists are primarily interested in the ways in which art develops within various social, political, and economic structures, and this necessitates an already established method of determining which things are works of art. In order to compare art, politics, and religion, for example, one must have already delineated the artistic, the political, and the religious. And in order to show how artworks in a capitalist society differ from artworks in a socialist society, one must already have identified the objects within each of these societies that count as art. We must separate here the search for an understanding of the way culture and society affect art from the search for a social or cultural definition of art. The same sort of problems for distinguishing art from nonart that arose in connection with attempts to define art in terms of 'function' arise here. Just as the failure to identify a unique function for art precludes our defining it in pragmatic terms, so failure to separate art off from all other institutions and sociopolitical activities precludes our defining it in these terms. As Wellek and Warren argue in their chapter on literature and society, the claim "literature is an expression of society" is wrong if the word 'correct' is added, and trivial if understood as saying that literature depicts some aspect of social reality:

[C]an we precisely define the influence of a book on its readers? Will it ever be possible to describe the influence of satire? Did Addison really change the manners of his society or Dickens incite reforms of debtors' prisons, boys' schools, and poorhouses? Was Harriet Beecher Stowe really the "little woman who made the great war"? Has *Gone with the Wind* changed Northern readers' attitudes towards Mrs. Stowe's war? How have Hemingway and Faulkner affected their readers? . . . The question, "How does literature affect its audience?" is an empirical one, to be answered, if at all, by the appeal to experience; and, since we are thinking of literature in the broadest sense, and society in the broadest, the appeal must be made to the experience not of the connoisseur alone but to that of the human race. We have scarcely begun to study such questions.[97]

Answering these empirical questions will, of course, provide us with a great deal that is interesting about the arts. But it will not prove that works of art are essentially cultural or social in nature.

Unlike sociologists of art, some Marxists are, of course, also interested in prescribing the way that art should be—in discovering principles of evaluation—not only in describing it as one institution among many. But these activities also presuppose, rather than give, a definition of art. As Edmund Wilson says, "The rules observed in any given school of art become apparent, not before, but after the actual works of art have been produced."[98]

Edmund Wilson himself was very sympathetic to the Marxist critical position, and although he became somewhat disenchanted with it later in his life, he remained convinced that it could explain a great deal about the social significance of art. Nonetheless, he is adamant in pointing out the weakness of Marxism both for evaluating and prescribing art. In *New Masses* of 1933 he quotes from Granville Hicks's list of requirements for the ideal Marxist work given in *The Crisis in Criticism*. Such a work must " 'lead the proletarian reader to recognize his role in the class struggle,' " and so must "(1) 'directly or indirectly show the effects of the class struggle,' (2) 'the author must be able to make the reader feel that he is participating in the lives described,' and (3) 'the author must have the viewpoint of the vanguard of the proletariat; he should be or should try to make himself, a member of the proletariat.' " Hicks adds that " 'no novel as yet written perfectly conforms to our demands.' "[99] The fact that no works of art produced heretofore conform to such demands shows how useless this kind of theorizing is for our problem of picking out art from nonart.

The most recent theories of art (in the analytic tradition) do use social or cultural concepts to define 'art'. These theories fall under the general name "institutional theories of art." Arthur Danto used the term 'artworld'[100] (a term based on ideas found in several of Harold Rosenberg's *New Yorker* articles) to refer to the complex social, cultural, political, and economic practices which center in our culture on the creation of art works. Never defined precisely, the artworld includes not just artists and the things they make, but museums,

aesthetic and artistic education, the publishing industry, governmental granting agencies, and committees making decisions about who gets funds and
which firms are awarded architectural contracts.

The most careful and clearest working out of such a definition of 'art' is
George Dickie's. Dickie's writing is always clear and so full of good common
sense that one cannot help but feel its appeal. Developed in a series of papers,
Dickie's theory is given the fullest treatment in a book entitled *Art and the
Aesthetic: An Institutional Analysis*. There he defines 'art' as follows: "A work
of art in the classificatory sense is (1) an artifact, (2) a set of the aspects of
which has had conferred upon it the status of candidate for appreciation by
some person or persons acting on behalf of a certain social institution (the
artworld)."[101] Status is conferred informally in the sense that there are no rigid
rules or lines of authority (as there are, for example, in making someone a
knight). It is something like christening, but, as in that situation, it is not
simply the case that saying makes it so. And Dickie continues, "Just as the
christening of a child has as its background the history and structure of the
church, conferring the status of art has as its background the Byzantine
complexity of the artworld."[102] Without this complex social and cultural
setting, objects do not and cannot become works of art:

> My thesis is that, in a way analogous to the way in which a person is
> certified as qualified for office, or two persons acquire the status of
> commonlaw marriage within a legal system, or a person is elected president
> of the Rotary, or a person acquires the status of wise man within a commu-
> nity, so an artifact can acquire the status of candidate for appreciation
> within the social system called "the artworld." How can one tell when the
> status has been conferred? An artifact's hanging in an art museum as part of
> a show and a performance at a theater are sure signs. There is, of course, no
> guarantee that one can always know whether something is a candidate for
> appreciation, just as one cannot always tell whether a given person is a
> knight or married. When an object's status depends upon nonexhibited
> characteristics a simple look at the object will not necessarily reveal that
> status. The non-exhibited relation *may* be symbolized by some badge, for
> example, by a wedding ring, in which a simple look will reveal the
> status.[103]

There is much that is sensible in Dickie's theories; as we shall see in the
next chapter, I myself am greatly indebted to his discussion. I, too, believe
that art cannot be understood outside of the context within which it comes to,
and continues to, exist. However, there are serious weaknesses with his
definition, as several people recently have been at pains to point out. (Indeed,
the great number of articles criticizing Dickie is the best evidence for the
influence of his work.) As Monroe Beardsley succinctly states, the most seri-

ous problems cluster about the failure of the theory to answer these questions: On what is the conferring done? What is conferred? Who does the conferring? What constitutes the conferring?[104]

The most thorough criticism of Dickie's definition of art comes from Ted Cohen, and I think we can do no better than to summarize it here. Cohen believes that the definition goes wrong in the second condition ("upon which some society or some sub-group of a society has conferred the status of candidate for appreciation"), the trouble being with "appreciation."[105] Dickie says that the kind of appreciation he has in mind is the kind characteristic of experiences of paintings, novels, and the like. Cohen thinks that there is no such kind of appreciation: "It seems to me it is . . . too much to suppose that there is a kind of appreciation characteristic of our experiences of, say, Rembrandt, Cézanne, Pollock, Olitski, 'and the like.'"[106] Dada, he contends, required a new kind of appreciation, and this makes lumping the appreciation of Rembrandt and Dada together a mistake. "This," he says, "suggests two things: (1) that being a candidate for appreciation in any but the emptiest sense of 'appreciation' (where it signifies any kind of apprehension to anything which is an artwork) is not part of what it is to be an artwork, at least not for some works, and (2) that possibilities concerning what *can* be appreciated have some bearing on what can be made a candidate for appreciation. The second point is not considered by Dickie, and this is responsible for what I think of as a formal gap in his definition."[107] In order for the theory to stand up we must understand the circumstances in which conferral is made and must be able to answer the question, "By whom?" Dickie does not describe the former and does not think the latter is a question: "In both art-making and candidate-making there exist constraints in terms of the objects. The head of the election board cannot make just anyone a candidate. Typically there will be a minimum age, a residence requirement, a stipulation that there be no criminal record, a requirement that there be nominating petitions signed by some number of registered voters, and so on."[108] But what are the corresponding stipulations and restrictions for art making? Dickie does not tell us.[109]

A related effort to define art in cultural or social terms is found in a paper by Joseph Margolis, in which he discusses the problem of the ontological status of works of art. He there suggests that works of art are entities that emerge culturally from the physical objects in which they are embodied. A statue, for example, is located in a block of stone, but as a statue it has properties that the stone by itself does not have. Statues can be angry; stones cannot. The possibility of attributing terms such as 'anger' to carved stones depends upon "artistic and appreciative traditions of a given culture."[110]

The way in which aesthetic properties emerge from physical objects is analogous, Margolis suggests, to the way in which certain human action descriptions emerge from bodily movements. "A man raises his arm to signal. . . . Apart from human society there is no such action, no more than a movement of the arm. . . ."[111] The efficiency of human society depends upon the ways in which rules turn physical movements and sounds into complex acts of communication. Ignorance of the rules can inconvenience us or even have dire consequences. Not knowing what a particular hand gesture means in a particular culture can be not only embarrassing, but dangerous. In analogous ways, physical objects become works of art, according to Margolis, and take on special attributes and meanings. And it is the existence of critical practices that support this metamorphosis. Apart from human society and cultures, stones cannot be angry or graceful or classical. According to Margolis, "It's clear that one's account of the nature of criticism and of the nature of a work of art are conceptually linked in the most intimate ways."[112]

It will become obvious in later chapters that Margolis and I are in complete agreement concerning the conceptual importance of critical activity. Unfortunately, Margolis does not give a specific account of what this conceptual link consists of; he merely says that the artistic and appreciative traditions are "rule-like regularities."

In one sense it is quite natural for Margolis to use the notion of "rule-like regularities" in his discussion. The role of 'rule' in recent philosophy has been prominent, especially in ethics, philosophy of language, and philosophy of science. It has been used with varying degrees of success by such distinguished thinkers as Rawls, Austin, Searle, and Kuhn to shed light on a wide range of philosophic problems. However, there are many kinds of rules, and philosophy still awaits a clear analysis of what a rule is and how it fits in these different contexts. It is not clear whether Margolis thinks the rules of tradition are more on the order of paradigms or constitutive rules. Do the rulelike regularities Margolis has in mind prescribe or describe the cultural behavior that surrounds objects identified as works of art? Is it a constitutive rule of the sort that one must serve underhand before one can be said to be playing badminton? Is this the kind of rule linking criticism and art? Or is describing stones in emotional terms ('angry', 'tender', 'triumphant') more closely analogous to suggesting strategy—"good rules to follow," for example, "It's best to serve high and deep or short and low, nothing in between." Unless Margolis more completely indicates what he means by "rule-like," use of this notion is a hedge which only makes matters more vague. As Beardsley says, he "does not tell us just what we must look for in the traditions in determining whether a particular object embodies a work of art."[113] And of course, this is precisely what we must know if we are to be able to distinguish art from nonart.

John M. Ellis has recently added a definition of 'literature' to the growing body of institutional analyses of art. He claims that if we understand what literary treatment of an object consists of, we have begun to get at the nature of literature. Instead of trying to generate a theory of literature by distilling properties or modes of organization common to all literary texts or attempting to discover some nature unique to authors, he believes we should begin by asking, "What circumstances are appropriate to the use of the word 'literature'?" and by looking for "features of those circumstances that determine the willingness of the speakers of the language to use the word."[114] 'Literature' is like 'weed', he claims; it is societal attitudes and performances which determine its application, not properties shared by a group of objects.

Ellis suggests the following as a definition: "Literary texts are defined as those that are used by the society in such a way that *the text is not taken as specifically relevant to the immediate context of its origin*."[115] But I am afraid that this is too broad. It would not distinguish literary texts from, say, political treatises or philosophic texts (with no redeeming literary value). Furthermore, Ellis maintains that when we view something like *The Decline and Fall of the Roman Empire* as literature, "Truth or falsity relevant to the specific historical context is no longer the main point, for Gibbon's is no longer the book for that purpose; we now read it as a narrative with its own kind of rationale."[116] But failure to consider truth-value in the context of origin does not provide the sufficient condition we need—else jokes would be literature, too. Additionally, truth and falsity may be very central to a work's "own rationale" without the work's failing to be literature. It is also difficult to imagine what rationale would be substituted for truth in Gibbon's opus—particularly if one wants to retain for it any connection with the author.

But even if we do not accept Ellis's definition of literature, we can accept his admonition to look at the way the term is applied, specifically at what speakers do when they apply it. In this chapter we have been doing exactly that with the term 'art'. We are about to turn to an attempt at constructing a theory of art based upon what we have discovered.

3

The Context of a Work of Art

In chapter 2 we considered several different ways in which properties not actually *in* the object are referred to in discussions of works of art. These references exemplify how often we are shown things we might otherwise miss. We can see that there is a man in the painting, but we may not know—indeed we cannot know, prior to having learned the customary symbolism of Western art—that the man is Jesus Christ. We recognize the Christ figure because a critic has explained that this is one, or because we have learned the special language of painting: we know that this sort of figure is generally a Christ. We may hear the musical notes at a concert, but it will not be obvious, without further contextual knowledge, that the composer is quoting from another's work.

Taken singly, the kinds of things critics refer to (the history of the work, the artist's intention or personal background) cannot form the basis from which an adequate method for distinguishing art from nonart can be developed. It is false that in each and every case we must know who is depicted in order to determine whether or not we have a painting before us. And the case is similar for other kinds of extrinsic facts: knowledge about who the artist is, what the artist's specific intentions were, or how the work has been interpreted in the past. At best we can claim that sometimes it helps to know the work's history, or only that in some cases it is essential that we know the artist's intentions.

But many philosophers, myself included, are uncomfortable with the indeterminacy of "sometimes" or "in some cases." I wish to suggest that the common denominator here lies in *the reference to the context of a work*. While none of these facts about art works can alone provide us with the means for defining 'work of art', taken together they do provide such a basis. I am claiming, then, that the context of a work of art is essential to its definition. Even if one grants that intrinsic, directly perceived properties are of primary importance in understanding and evaluating a work of art, it is only when the objects to which these properties are attributed are attended to within a certain context that they can be identified as properties of a work of art. We could thus spell out the relationship of 'work of art' to 'context' in predicate language this way: the predicate 'work of art' is a two-place predicate in which a certain sort of object, x, is related to a context, y. This definition is, however, unsatisfactory. It is not enough simply to say that the predicate 'is a work of art' is a two-place predicate in which some sort of object is related to some sort of context. This leaves the particular nature of the relationship between the object and its context completely unspecified, and hence is so broad that it is of little or no use in answering specific questions about the status of an object. Many difficulties with intentionalist theories of art, for example, suffer from this kind of vagueness. It may be true that an object is a work of art only if it is the result of intentional activity; but one feels compelled to ask, "So what?" unless particular features of the object and particular intentions are tied together in each and every art work.

One way of specifying the relation between an object and its context is in terms of a particular causal connection, and I would like to suggest the following revision: The predicate 'work of art' is a two-place predicate in which an object is related to its history of production. This limits the contextual features to be considered to those which have to do with factors referred to by critics and historians that relate to the creation or production of an object— the sorts of extrinsic facts we looked at in chapter 2. (I shall say more later about the terms 'context' and 'history of production'.) The statement still suffers from broadness—indeed, it is an even more general statement than the intentionalist theorist makes, and we have already found that to be too broad to be of much use to us. In the next chapter, I shall narrow this second definition in such a way that it becomes a practical and useful theory.

But first we must look more fully into what it means to say that the phrase 'work of art' is a two-place predicate. Many predicates (or property names)[1] are such that they are attributed to one object at a time. Words or phrases such as 'is a man', 'is a country', 'is tall', or 'is smiling' result in perfectly sensible statements when the name or description of a single item is placed before them: *"Paul Newman* is a man, " *"Denmark* is a country," *"The richest person in the room* is tall," or *"The Virgin in the picture* is smiling." Since only one place need be filled in order for us to get a meaningful statement, these are called "one-place predicates".

Other predicates require that two or more things be named in order for them to result in a meaningful sentence—'is to the north of', for instance, or 'is between', 'is taller than', 'is thinking about', or 'is the uncle of'. We utter nonsense if, naming or describing only one entity, we say, "Denmark is to the north of," "Tom is between," "The richest person in the room is taller than," "The Virgin in the picture is thinking about," or "My brother is the uncle of." Some of these predicates require that one more thing be named, say 'Denmark' and 'Italy', or 'the richest person in the room' and 'the poorest person in the room', or 'the Virgin' and 'Jesus', or 'my brother' and 'my son'. And some predicates, for example, 'is between', require that three things be named, as in "*Tom* is between *Joe* and *Dennis*." All of these predicates name or specify a relation that exists between the things named, and hence can be called "relative" terms. The term 'work of art' as I use it above, then, is such a relative term.

But it is important here to distinguish between the ways in which the term 'relative' may be used. Problems arise in connection with such statements as "Raw oysters taste good," for they can be both asserted and denied of the same raw oysters; and determining whether it is the assertion or the denial that is true, independent of reference to the speaker, is impossible. It is thus claimed that the sentence is true or false "relative" to the subject who is making the judgment. Hence it is often said that this kind of statement is "relative" or "subjective." Yet it does not necessarily follow that the statement lacks a truth-value (is neither true nor false) as some philosophers have concluded. For one can use the sentence to lie, deceive, joke, be ironic, and pretend, all actions which, when verbal, depend upon the sentence's having a truth-value. For example, in order to present himself as a sophisticated gourmet, Jones may decide to pretend to like raw oysters. So he says, "Raw oysters taste good." The pretense can succeed only if what Jones says is taken to be something which he believes to be true; it simply will not work if Jones and/or his hearers believe that this sentence is incapable of carrying truth-value. Nevertheless, the problem remains that Smith, during the same conversation, can say "Raw oysters do not taste good," and not produce the obvious contradiction that will result if Jones and Smith, again during the same conversation, say respectively, "Oysters live in cold water" and "Oysters do not live in cold water." The terms "relativity" and "subjectivity" have thus been used to distinguish judgmental statements like the ones about the taste of oysters from the "objective" or "absolute" statements about their living habits.

To maintain that the term 'work of art' is "relative" is not necessarily to conclude that it is relative in the sense of being indeterminate, or a mere matter of subjective opinion. 'X is a work of art' is on a par with 'x is an uncle' or 'x is hungry'. 'Is hungry' and 'is an uncle' have truthfully been both asserted and denied of my brother. This is not contradictory, as one might suppose, since completion of a predicate like 'is hungry' will involve a specification of a particular time or a particular object of hunger:

My brother is hungry at 5:30, 15 January 1978. (True)
My brother is hungry at 6:30, 15 January 1978. (False)

My brother is hungry for chocolate ice cream. (True)
My brother is hungry for raw oysters. (False)

Completion of 'is an uncle' consists of specifying a particular kinship system (as well, again, as a time). Thus my brother may be an uncle in the United States, but not in some South Pacific island society. Once we complete the predicates we can clearly determine their truth-value, and no contradiction will result.

But it is not always immediately obvious whether a predicate has one or more places. 'Is a refrigerator' appears to be monadic. Yet we can imagine a Frigidaire shipped to an island with no electricity. Is that Frigidaire a refrigerator or not? One might argue that being a refrigerator is relative to the availability of electricity and that the question "Is it a refrigerator or isn't it?" cannot be answered as it stands, any more than "Is it to the north or not?" can be answered without first answering, "North of what?"

The choice of the examples above—'is hungry', 'is an uncle', and 'is a refrigerator'—was not arbitrary. Each predicate involves a different type of relation, and each has an analog in aesthetic theory. As we have already seen, various aesthetic or artistic theories emphasize one or more of these (and other) kinds of relations. We might, for instance, compare the predicate 'is hungry' to the sorts of artistic theories that emphasize the importance of how a person feels in the presence of a work of art for determining whether or not the work is indeed an artistic object. Just as someone's being hungry or not depends upon how she or he feels at that particular moment, so a work of art might be defined as such if a particular person feels at that moment that it is one.

As we saw in chapter 2, some of the most recent developments in aesthetics surround theories in which being a work of art is thought to depend upon the existence of certain social or cultural institutions; such theories liken 'is a work of art' to 'is an uncle'. In our kinship system we have natural uncles and uncles by marriage. Just as the latter kind of "uncleship" depends upon the existence of institutions and actions within those institutions which connect people not related biologically—depends on one's connection to some other person within a kinship network—so, according to such theories, being a work of art depends upon actions performed within existing institutions. Thus

George Dickie defines art as an artifact presented to an artworld as a candidate for appreciation; works of art, he says, are essentially dubbed as such by a complicated system of unwritten rules that somehow confer the status of 'work of art'.

And finally, it has been argued that an object qualifies as a work of art only if it is possible for the object to function in certain ways. Like the refrigerator, its existence is relative to the possibility of its functioning in a certain fashion. An essential feature of art, say these theorists, is its publicity, accessibility, and/or repeatability; and historians and critics in laboring to teach viewers how to read works aid in making this feature possible. The existence of viewers who understand the symbol system in which a work of art has been created is analogous to the availability of electricity for the refrigerator.

I hope to show that contextual features explain how art differs from nonart. So far I have said very little about what I mean by 'context', other than that I believe the predicate 'work of art' relates an object to its history of production. Like 'context', 'history of production' (about which more will be said below) is broad, and must remain so. In chapter 2 we looked at a variety of references to contextual features, and in chapter 4 we shall see how these are involved in a specific definition of 'work of art'. Here I want to indicate how context can be used in aesthetic theories by showing how one philosopher, Arthur Danto, uses a particular kind of contextual feature to explain how one sort of art differs from another. I have chosen Danto's work as an example because he shares my view that the term 'work of art' is relative in the sense outlined above.

In a very interesting article entitled "The Transfiguration of the Common-place," Danto discusses problems involved in distinguishing representational works from nonrepresentational ones.[2] He asks us to consider a blank canvas hanging in a museum. There is a difference between the artist's calling the work "Untitled" and its being a matter of fact that the artist did not give the work a title, even though in both cases the work may be referred to in the catalog as "Untitled." The artist may respond, "Nothing," when asked what the work is about. This response is similarly ambiguous. It may be that the work is about nothing or there may be nothing that it is about. We cannot, in these examples, know whether the terms 'untitled' or 'nothing' are proper names or descriptions of the works until we know the causes for those terms appearing in the catalog. Thus Danto concludes that "one sort of condition for something to be in candidacy for interpretation, title, and structure will be certain assumptions with regard to its causes. And causes are not the sort of things we can read off the surfaces. . . ."[3]

This is also true, Danto argues, for distinguishing representational from nonrepresentational works. We know already from Gombrich and Goodman that resemblance is not sufficient to distinguish these.[4] What is also essential, according to Danto, is that a work be *about* that of which it is a representation. "Imagine," he says, "a man who dresses and acts the way women in a given society dress and act. Mere resemblance in habit and gait will not as such make of him a female impersonator, for he may by accidental circumstance believe that this is just the way one dresses and acts, perhaps because, like the young Achilles, he is brought up with women and affects their dress and manner. . . . We all imitate our models, but do not impersonate them unless our imitating is also *about* what is imitated. . . ."[5] It is possible that no intrinsic property of x distinguishes it from y, and yet for x to be a portrait and y not a portrait; again it is *being about* that is the essential distinguishing fact.

Danto analyzes the above relation as follows:

A is about B if and only if A denotes B and A is causally related to B.

That is, denotation and causation are necessary and sufficient conditions for one thing's being about another. Portraits denote and are causally related to the persons they are portraits of. This analysis also explains why cloud formations cannot be *about* little dogs, the Taj Mahal or witches' faces, although they may look like them. In order for a resemblance to be about that which it resembles, there must be a causal connection, and it is this, of course, which is missing in cloud formations.

Danto's analysis is relevant to the discussion here for this reason. Although, as I have pointed out, his main interest is in representation, I believe his position can be generalized and thought of as suggesting a means for distinguishing works of art from non–works of art. Because of his interest in imitation, Danto focuses on situations in which a work has the appearance it has due to (because of) an artist's putting paint on a canvas in a certain manner as a consequence of what he sees. But we can broaden his approach to include other things that determine the internal properties of works of art. A work's context or history of production is not limited to the visual experience of the artist. Just as Danto uses this one feature of the context, linking what an artist has seen and the object he or she consequently creates, to differentiate representational from nonrepresentational art, we can use a set of contextual features—what I have called features in an object's 'history of production'—to distinguish objects that are works of art from ones that are not. This set of features includes the variety of things we looked at in chapter 2: artistic technique, biography, content, cultural conditions, and consequences. One might believe that the orange crate A was not the result of an artist's attempting to recreate what he saw, and yet still insist that it is a work of art only if it has a special sort of history, for instance, if the artist had certain expressive intentions.

It may seem odd to include under the general term 'history of production' factors which do not precede, but follow, a work. One might wonder, for instance, how we could maintain that a work's *consequences* are part of its history. The advantage of the term is that by including the words 'history' and 'production', it becomes clear that reference to extrinsic properties is legitimate. 'History' here is to refer not only to the way (how, why, when, and so on) the work itself came into being, but to its whole *story*—what happened to it, what effects it had on its viewers, as well as its genesis. Thus we might also include "consequences" of the sort Oscar Cargill discusses in the following passage:

> The two books by Bourget which are of consequence to us, because they provoked *The Golden Bowl* and provided certain important elements in its plot, are *Cosmopolis* (1893) and *A Tragic Idyl* (1896). *Cosmopolis*, as a work of art, is distinguished by a rigorous adherence to a point of view in a fashion which would have delighted Henry James, all of the events of the story falling within the cognizance of Julien Dorsenne, a successful young French novelist living in Rome, whose natural good instincts are warped and perverted by a cosmopolitan cynicism which he adopts.[6]

We find here references to the consequences of Bourget's novels and to the causes of James's novel, artistic attitudes, and current views of culture and society.

None of these contextual properties can alone be used to support a theory of art. Nonetheless, I am struck by the obvious relevance of referring to some features of an object's history of production. It is difficult to find a single discussion of an artwork which does not, for example, mention works by other artists. Discussion about influence and artistic development demands this. Obviously, it is possible to discuss a work without mentioning other works; such discussions do exist. But even these use a special vocabulary, one that presupposes an understanding of certain concepts whose meanings have developed in and through the traditions of art history and criticism. And these, we have seen, are full of reference to things beyond the intrinsic properties of a single work under consideration.

I am not claiming that I have, in the preceding chapter, exhausted all the possible aspects of histories of production to which a writer might refer; I hope, simply, to assert the relevance of those extrinsic facts I have examined. Of course, once the relevance of reference to properties lying outside of a given work has been admitted, only part of the question has been answered.

For, as we have seen, it is easy to disagree about which nonintrinsic properties matter. Further difficulty results from the fact that the particular type of nonintrinsic property referred to in one instance may not be helpful in another. Thus being told, "Picasso did it," in the example of the orange crate may give one pause, whereas being told, "Roberta Peters did it," in the case of the moose call, may not matter at all.

Nor am I claiming that reference to history of production is unique to discussions about works of art. When Walter Havighurst describes the development of Mississippi waterways, he gives us the following kind of information:

> For twenty years, while river traffic grew and carting cargoes around the falls became Louisville's chief business, men talked of a canal. At last in 1825 the Louisville and Portland Company went to work. They dug a mile-long ditch across Louisville's river front, past the old landing of Shipping-port to Portland, then a separate town, rejoining the river abreast of Sandy Island. Work began in 1825 with gangs of slaves manning shovels and wheelbarrows. In December, 1830, the steamboat *Uncas* locked through to a clangor of bells and boom of cannon. At tolls of twenty cents per ton for steamboats and four dollars for flatboats, the canal made fortunes for its builders and spurred the river trade. By 1840 fifteen hundred steamboats and hundreds of keels and flatboats passed through the locks each year.[7]

And Robert Riegel in describing railroads says,

> Another important factor toward the development of uniform gauge [of railroad tracks] was the rapid improvement in bridge building. The first bridge over the Mississippi south of St. Paul was built by the Mississippi and Missouri River (Chicago and Rock Island) and was comparable in importance to the Niagara suspension bridge, finished about the same time. The first contracts were let in 1853 and the entire 1535 feet of bridge was opened for traffic three years later. It marked the beginning of a new era in western transportation even though it was another decade before an additional bridge was opened.[8]

In these passages the authors point not only to intrinsic properties, but also to the intention with which the structures were produced, public reaction, method of production, function, consequences, and relations to other works of the same kind. Thus the presence of reference to history of production does not itself serve to differentiate descriptions of art objects from nonart objects.

Does this failure to differentiate artistic objects from ordinary ones result in a skepticism which is so fundamental to the identification of something as a work of art that it ultimately serves as a logical or epistemological basis for distinguishing art from nonart? We have no trouble recognizing the orange crate as an orange crate, but it often appears that we cannot finally settle the question concerning its status as a work of art. Are art objects unique in that they are the sort of thing about which some people say, "Yes, it is," and others say, "No, it is not"?

Let us return briefly to the refrigerator example. Surely, we might claim, everyone knows what refrigerators are. We have no trouble, for example, distinguishing them from the dishwashers in appliance stores. But the point of imagining a refrigerator on an unelectrified island was to show that we can be made to doubt even our ability to distinguish refrigerators from non-refrigerators. A clever enough philosopher might even cook up a story in which we are not finally certain whether something is really, truly, an orange crate or not. Of course, once we have admitted that external factors (like the context of the refrigerator) matter and have further decided that, in particular, the presence of electricity makes the difference, we can settle the refrigerator question. We could decide to call things "refrigerators" only if there is a source of electricity within reach that allows them to fulfill the function of refrigerating. Or we could decide to call them refrigerators if there is a source of electricity somewhere in the world that would allow them to refrigerate. The point is that a decision could be reached which would resolve the indeterminacy. Once we've made analogous decisions for the orange crate and moose call, we will similarly have answered our questions about their status as works of art. Hence, the difficulty of determining whether an object belongs to a certain class or not does not provide a means of logically or epistemologically separating art objects from non–art objects.

Suppose people–not just philosophers but people prominent enough in the public eye to attract attention and publicity–made their living by getting us to wonder whether something is a refrigerator or not. If you can imagine this, it shouldn't surprise you that the argument in the sculpture garden goes on, for many contemporary artists do have as a central goal the casting of just such doubt.

Perhaps it would be wise to stop here for a moment and decide whether there is any good reason for answering the question this book poses. What possible difference can it make whether 'refrigerator' can truly be predicated of something on an unelectrified island or not? Why should anyone care whether it is correct or incorrect to describe an orange crate or a moose call as a 'work of art'?

We can create at least a farfetched story to account for the importance of settling the refrigerator question. The beloved chieftain on our unelectrified island has been kidnapped by a tribe from a neighboring electrified island. In the ransom note the delivery of one refrigerator is demanded in return for her

Fig. 12. Carl Andre, *Stone Field.* **Connecticut Department of Economic Development.**

safety. Do we have something to send? We can make up a similar story for the orange crate. The neighboring tribe demands two art works in return for the chieftain's safety. Should we send both orange crates A and B, only one, or neither?

If no case for the relevance of this issue can be made independently of such fairy tales, it must be an insignificant matter. However, I believe we can give stronger reasons in support of its significance. There are, first of all, genuine practical concerns. Which objects are to be given space in museums? Which museums should we support with public funds? How can we ensure truth in concert advertising? What do we put in public gardens? Which objects are to be included in courses on art appreciation?

In August 1977, a sculptural complex entitled "Stone Field Sculptures" was installed in a downtown public green in Hartford, Connecticut (See figure *12.*) The sculpture consisted of thirty-six glacial boulders weighing from one thousand pounds to eleven tons. Many citizens of Hartford were outraged that a "bunch of rocks" could pass as a legitimate work of art. Efforts were even made to hold up payment of the artist, Carl Andre. Meetings were held to discuss possible removal of the stones. According to Andre, "There was a lot of real hostility during the installation. . . . People would come up and start screaming at me—really screaming. People from all social and economic classes. I was quite startled by the vehemence. Now I suspect they were just using this as a vent for their rage in other areas, sort of a handy target. Nobody's *that* interested in art."[9] Perhaps no one is *that* interested in art, but clearly there is more than passing interest in what passes under the name 'work of art'. In Hartford, for example, one mayoral candidate objected that money spent for the sculpture was "another slap in the face for the poor and elderly."[10]

There are other concerns of a more theoretical nature centering on problems of interpretation and evaluation. Anything *can* be viewed from the "aesthetic point of view"—whatever that is. But art objects *should* be so viewed. If I believe that something is a work of art, chances are I will view it differently than if I believe it is merely an orange crate. "Differently" here may simply amount to looking for things I probably would not otherwise have looked for. Nelson Goodman makes a related point in his discussion of art forgeries. The fact that we are unable now to distinguish between a fraud and the real thing does not mean that we will always be unable to distinguish between them. And the belief that an object is, in fact, the real thing will, Goodman thinks, make us scrutinize it more carefully than we would otherwise have done.[11]

I hope by now to have established two fundamental points. (1) Critics, historians, and theorists bring us to perceive things about works that we might, on our own, have missed. (2) And they often do this by referring to the context or history of production of the work. In the next chapter these two points will generate a theory of art.

4

The Theory

We saw in chapter 2 that as we engage in the activity of interpreting or evaluating a work of art, we give more consideration to some features of an artistic object or event than others. And critical discussion, as we have seen, plays a large part in focusing our attention in this way; critics and theorists often select for us those facts they consider most important, those features we are to give the most attention. But no single, critical tactic, providing facts about the artist's life or the cultural setting of the work, for instance, gave us a foundation on which to build a definition of 'work of art'. How can we determine for certain whether cultural information will be relevant? Some kinds of historical facts seem more important than others. Properties that seem important to the interpretation of one work seem irrelevant even to other works of the same kind. Nonetheless, I think that we can at least postulate the following claim: we can say that reference to a work's extrinsic properties is important and relevant when it directs us back to the work itself, to the intrinsic properties of a work. The fact that Goya was deaf or Bartók lonely will not be of much help to us when we consider their work unless this information is related back to the work's intrinsic properties, those properties considered important in interpretation and evaluation. Extrinsic fact "A" is more important than fact "B" if "A" leads us back to the work to concentrate on relevant sets of internal properties, while "B" sheds no real light on the original object. This also provides us with a way of identifying the properties relevant to evaluation within a particular aesthetic school or tradition. And both of these ways of relating information concerning history of production to aesthetic activity are central to the definition of 'work of art' that I shall develop in this and the next chapter.

Can it be that our ability to perceive a property depends upon the descriptions which critics give us? We might agree that less than ideal observers need help, that *in practice* historians and critics bring us to a fuller perception of the works of art we encounter. But does it follow from this that perceivable properties are tied *in theory* to the identification of a work of art? Of course, it might be admitted, some people might not see the ship in the background of Géricault's *Raft of the Medusa* (see plate I), and hence will fail to appreciate fully the physical and psychological action the artist chose to represent. But isn't it possible to see this sort of thing without help from anyone? And doesn't it follow that in principle we can perceive all of the intrinsic properties of an object without being given any extrinsic information about its history of production? I believe that identifying what we are contemplating as a work of art does lead us to concentrate on properties we would not normally consider if we were viewing an everyday object—an orange crate, say.

Some ways of describing objects do depend upon that object's having been identified as a special kind of thing. I cannot look at a piece of stone and see a pedestal, for example, if I am not looking at a statue or a column. I believe that the term 'work of art' acts as 'statue' or 'column' in this case: not only is identifying an object as a work of art and providing information about its history of production *useful* in bringing us to a fuller perception of it, it is, at least sometimes, *necessary* to a full perception of its aesthetic properties. The decision to treat something as a work of art then, has enormous consequences.

We are probably unaware of just how much both critical commentary and general exposure to critical ideas affect the way we view works of art. It is a commonplace of contemporary psychology that our expectations guide our perceptions. The knowledge, beliefs, attitudes, and habits that we bring with us to new situations determine to a great extent the new experience itself by drawing our attention to details we anticipate or expect to be crucial. As we saw in chapter 2, there are many ways in which information about a work's history of production affects our perception of it. Both the range and effect of these expectations is enormous. We are given a multitude of information about the works we encounter—in reviews, critical works, in the words of more knowledgeable friends. And we have larger expectations about works of art as well. We expect them to be studied, appreciated, admired; we expect to be able to react to them in certain ways.

Perhaps the most familiar instance of how our expectations guide our experience with a work of art is the case of a person who reads divergent interpretations of the same work. Having studied Robert Heilman's religious analysis of *The Turn of the Screw*, a reader will suddenly notice all the internal details relevant to this reading (even items Heilman failed to mention): the repetition of the word 'divine', perhaps, the devilish characteristics of Peter Quint, or the priestly metaphors with which the governess describes herself. But should this same reader subsequently read another interpretation, say Edmund Wilson's Freudian analysis, and reapproach the novel, religious details will seem to fade somewhat in significance, and new details gain prominence: Flora making a boat by sticking one piece of wood into another, Quint's appearance on a tower, Miss Jessel's appearance across a lake, or the opening line of the governess's narration: "I remember the whole beginning as a succession of flights and drops, a little see-saw of the right throbs and the wrong." We reread with new and different insights.[1]

Of course, more general information about a work of art will also affect how we "read" it. Information we often take for granted, knowledge about a particular period or culture, for example, will have a tremendous impact on our aesthetic judgments. Language we would criticize for being "stilted" if it were written in 1980 is not vulnerable to the same criticism if we know we are dealing with a sixteenth-century play. Similarly, our attribution of predicates like 'lacks perspective', 'has dull colors', 'is unrealistic', 'is nonnatural', 'uses unimaginative camera placement', depends upon our knowing something about the work's context, depends on the different expectations we bring to works of different periods, different traditions, different genres.

Finally, we bring to any contemplation of a work of art a further, even more general, kind of expectation, one that will be crucial to our definition of 'work of art'. That is, even the very general expectation that what we are about to consider is a work of art and not some other sort of thing affects the way in which we perceive it. We know when we view a painting in a museum, for example, that we should look at brush strokes, but that there is no need to look at the reverse side of the canvas. It is impossible to specify completely all those properties that suddenly become relevant.

I suggest that we identify objects belonging to the class designated by the term 'work of art' as follows:

> x is a work of art if and only if (1) x is an artifact and (2) x is discussed in such a way that information concerning the history of production of x directs the viewer's attention to properties which are worth attending to.

Obviously, there are a great many concepts in this definition which require detailed attention. Let us first consider the complicated principle of artifactuality in further detail.

That artifactuality is a necessary condition of an object's being a work of art is now widely agreed upon. Thus Ted Cohen, in his article on George Dickie's institutional theory of art, while finding several important points to criticize (see chapter 2, section vii), simply accepts Dickie's condition of artifactuality without discussion. I have myself argued for the necessity of this condition elsewhere,[2] but the issue is important enough to merit repetition of that argument here.

According to the *Funk and Wagnalls New Standard Dictionary of the English Language* (1973), an artifact is "anything made or modified by human art." One argument that has been given (for example, by Henry Aiken)[3] is that 'work of art' carries the condition of artifactuality simply because the term includes the word 'work.' That is, is something has already been identified as a 'work', we presuppose that it is the result or product of some conscious or intentional human activity. This line of reasoning is supported by Funk and Wagnalls' definition of a 'work': "that which is produced by labor." An artifact, being a man-made object, is surely something produced by labor. Unfortunately, Funk and Wagnalls go on to say that a 'work' is "especially a product of nature or of art." But an artifact cannot be a product of nature. Thus I think we cannot rely too heavily on the presence of the word 'work'.

The condition of artifactuality is best approached, I think, by seeing how it is involved as a defining condition in another sort of concept. Consider the following (fictional) story. During World War II, a German colonel once had a tree in the yard of a house he occupied cut down because, he insisted, it was making the Allies' "V for Victory" sign. We can imagine what that poor, frail sapling must have looked like. The colonel's reason for wanting it destroyed was, of course, insane. But it was insane only if what bothered him was the belief that the tree itself was giving the victory sign. If instead he feared that the tree was being used as a symbol or substitute for the sign by the villagers—they looked at each other across the tree or just barely nodded or pointed in its direction as they passed—his state of mind and his action become more understandable; we could then call his actions futile, perhaps, but not insane.

A V-shape itself is not a 'V' until it comes to be used as such. So it is with the shape of words. It is difficult to construct examples that are not farfetched. But imagine pieces of driftwood lying on a beach. Wind and wave have arranged the individual pieces in the configuration: *Tidal wave in 1 hour*. If we come across the configuration during a walk on the beach, I may say to you, "Look, the driftwood *says* there will be a tidal wave in one hour." The use of 'says' here would probably not be incorrect. But that it is metaphoric becomes more apparent when we compare the term to 'warns', for surely it would be both literally and metaphorically incorrect to say, "Look, the driftwood is warning us that there will be a tidal wave in one hour." To warn is to perform what is now commonly called a "speech-act." Austin,[4] Searle,[5] and others have discussed such actions in detail. Suffice it to say here that speech-acts can be performed successfully only when certain conditions involving the speaker, hearer, and the situation in which the speech is made are fulfilled. One necessary condition for a successful (or as Austin says, "felicitous") warning is that the warner have a special intention, namely the intention to alert someone to something. Upon seeing the driftwood, we might conclude that *someone* is warning us that there will be a tidal wave in one hour. But the driftwood is not in itself warning or a warning; it is simply being used to warn. As such, the driftwood arranged by wind and wave into the configuration "Tidal wave in 1 hour" is nothing but a configuration. Under certain circumstances (say I hear on the radio that a tidal wave has developed and will hit shore in one hour and I use the configuration to warn a friend who is behind me, while I run on ahead down the beach to warn others), I can use the configuration to warn. Then and only then is it correct to say that the configuration has become a warning.

The driftwood here is analogous to the natural objects we sometimes regard as works of art. There is some controversy in aesthetics as to whether such objects do, indeed, ever deserve to be regarded as artistic objects. But the argument dissolves when we distinguish between natural objects in a natural setting and natural objects that are put to some aesthetic purpose. Lying untouched by human hand or unseen by the human eye, the driftwood is not a work of art. In order for it to become a work of art it must be used as one. Something must be done to it—it must be picked up, taken home and put on the mantel, for example. When we give it this new context, we change or modify the piece of driftwood. It is no longer as it was in its purely natural state. It has then become an artifact.

But, it will be objected, suppose we have two identical pieces of lava, one in a museum of natural history, one in a museum of contemporary art. Is the first a natural object and the second an artifact? Surely this is counterintuitive. Just putting something in a museum or on a mantel cannot make an artifact out of a natural object.

It is true, of course, that both pieces of lava have acquired new settings. And it is also true that the composition of neither object has changed. But only in the case of the piece of lava in the natural history museum is the way it was in its natural state of primary importance and interest to us. In a museum of contemporary art or on my mantel, however, it is the object's appearance which is the primary concern. Whether or not the natural object is now, strictly speaking, an artifact, it is being used and treated as such—as if it were a product of human rather than natural activity.

We can use the same kind of reasoning to explain "accidental" art works—"found poems," for instance. We are familiar with being asked to imagine monkeys sitting at typewriters randomly creating "great works" of art. Let us

also imagine writing poems according to the instructions of Lewis Carroll's
"Poeta Fit, Non Nascitur":

> For first you write a sentence,
>   And then you chop it small,
> Then mix the bits, and sort them out
>   Just as they chance to fall:
> The order of the phrases makes
>   No difference at all.[6]

Ordinarily, warning takes the form of uttering or writing words. Extraordinarily, it can take the form of using words or shapes that already exist (our driftwood configuration on the beach). Ordinarily, writing poetry takes the form of writing words. Extraordinarily, it too might take the form of using words or shapes that already exist. We could thus write poetry by taking sentences written by someone else, chopping them up, and then letting the pieces fall by chance. But by neither this method nor by the method of giving a monkey a typewriter have I done all that is required to make a poem. Like the driftwood, something has to be done with or to the shapes that result before they become a work of art. The modification that occurs in this case is my noticing or perceiving that some of the results produced in these random manners are poetry. For it is, of course, false that "the order of the phrases makes no difference at all." I choose only some pieces of driftwood to take home. I take up only some arrangements of letters and words and send them off to *Atlantic Monthly* in the hope that they will be published. What makes the difference, why I choose some random configurations and not others, remains to be seen. But when I do make my choices, I expose the object to all the critical commentary, all the interpretation that nonnatural aesthetic objects are subject to. What is important here is that natural objects, in order to become works of art, have to undergo some change or modification—and when we change or modify a natural object, or make something out of it in such a way that obviously involves human activity, some human choices, we have an artifact.

It is, I believe, because artifactuality is so crucial to an object's being a work of art, that the intentionalist position has its appeal. There is a clear relationship between a thing's being an artifact and its coming into existence as a result of certain human intentions. The notion of action in general, and speech-acts in particular, involves the existence of intentions on the part of the agent performing the action. Words, if they are really words and not simply shapes or sounds, are produced intentionally. Individual types of speech-acts, such as warnings or assertions, result only when the speaker has

Fig. 13. Berthel Thorvaldsen, *Christ*. Thorvaldsen's Museum, Copenhagen.

certain intentions—the intention to alert or to inform, for example. Mere change or modification of a natural object (for example picking up a piece of driftwood or throwing pieces of paper with marks on them) does not create an artifact. Certain intentions must be present: something is done with or to the driftwood or words for some reason.[7]

Frequently, the knowledge that something is man-made both makes us appreciate it and concentrate more fully upon it. The marble in the drapery in Thorvaldsen's *Christ* is incredibly thin. (See figure 13.) As human beings we appreciate the accomplishments of other human beings. Hence there is a tremendous difference in the way we react to Thorvaldsen's product and (imagining one exists) to a similar piece of marble made equally thin by forces of nature. When I said to my son, "Look how thin the sculptor made the marble here," I caused him to appreciate the artist's virtuosity, to attend to an intrinsic property that he had overlooked. His own sense of how difficult it is for a person to cut and polish a rock made that now-perceived property an occasion of heightened appreciation. When we treat an object as an artifact, we thus heighten its "perceivability."

But artifactuality has further implications as well. Taking something to be a work of art automatically implies that we somehow set it aside for appreciation. And if the object is to be available for discussion, for this heightened appreciation, it must be publicly accessible for some period of time. Otherwise there would be no way of distinguishing art from, say, tools. It is not that works of art cannot be "useful"; functional objects are not necessarily nonart. But an object whose value derives solely from its function, or from some other extrinsic property, is not a work of art. If it were, the object could be replaced by another object fulfilling the same function, with no sense of loss. An artifact, then, is available, set apart from ordinary objects. In order for the critical discussion—the discussion so crucial to its existence and definition—to occur, a work of art must be public property in some sense.

Of course, the concept of artifactuality must be broadened to include not just discrete objects, but actions as well (dancing, putting fences across California). But here we must note that only *accessible* actions may qualify. This means that in order to be accessible, such actions must be repeatable and/or documentable. In the first case a notation (score, directions for movements) must exist which allows for repetition of the action—and hence for some discussion of it. In the case of documented "happenings," the document really becomes the work of art itself, once the action has ended.

Perhaps we should pause briefly here to answer a possible objection. It might be argued that one cannot claim, for example, that when Bach improvised fugues and did not write them down he was not producing works of art even though they cannot now be repeated. The same is clearly true of jazz improvisations in our own day. Wasn't there music in the Ancient world even though no notation existed which permits us to play today what they played then?

In answer to this sort of objection we might say that in each of these cases it is *in principle* possible that these works could have been repeated. Works are passed on either intact (as in the case of paintings and statues) or through oral traditions or systems of notations (as in poems and songs), when those traditions or systems capture enough important features to allow us to identify instances of the same work.[8] But when no such traditions or systems exist which make duplication possible, as in the case of paintings, the work is gone forever when it is destroyed. The fugues Bach improvised that were not written down no longer exist either. But when he played them they could, in principle, have been written down and so were works of art at the time.

The same is true of jazz improvisation. It cannot be claimed that its value depends upon its not being repeatable. We do have and value many of Bach's and modern jazzists' recorded improvisations. And as we listen we do, of course, value the fact that the artist is creating the piece as he or she goes along. But it is not part of our appreciating that we believe it could not *possibly* be repeated.

Suppose that in an extended case of the "lost chord," an artist composes a piece as he plays, is struck with amnesia, and cannot repeat it. Suppose all art were like this, The artist might say, "I know I created a work of art, but I don't remember anything about it." If it were literally true that artists (and all others) remembered *nothing* about what was created, then, of course, we could not have a distinct, identifiable class of works of art. If we do remember *some* things, then those things can be reproduced more and more approximately.

The extreme amnesia case, then, suggests that having systems of notation, oral traditions, and other transcriptions such as photographic and phonographic recordings, is a practical rather than theoretical criterion. If our memories were perfect, these would be superfluous. But *repeatability*, as we shall see, is a theoretical requirement tied to the criterion of discussability.

The need to have repeatable access to art objects (and to the object in the state intended by the creator) is behind what many of us see as a need to put restrictions on the notion of "property rights" when the property is a work of art.[9] Carl R. Baldwin insists that a person who abhors a particular school of painting should not be allowed to buy a work simply in order to destroy it. He urges legislation in the United States similar to what is called in Europe, "le droit moral d'auteur." Perhaps "aesthetic right" would be a better term here, for it amounts to establishing a work's "immunity from any alteration that damages its character, and, thereby, the artist's reputation and financial prospects":

> In 1964, Buffet decorated the interior panel of a refrigerator that was slated to be auctioned off for some charitable purpose. The auctioneer however, held one panel in reserve, and attempted to sell it separately. Buffet complained, and the court found in his favor: since the work was conceived as a whole, no one had the right to separate one part from the other, and thereby to destroy the ensemble effect.[10]

Such a law thus insures the accessibility and hence the perceivability of a work of art, properties which accompany artifactuality.

Unfortunately, like intention (which, as we saw in chapter 2, does not alone support a definition of art), artifactuality does not suffice to solve our problem completely. George Kubler begins *The Shape of Time* by saying, "Let us suppose that the idea of art can be expanded to embrace the whole range of man-made things, including all tools and writing in addition to the useless, beautiful, and poetic things of the world. By this view the universe of man-made things simply coincides with the history of art."[11] But Kubler himself distinguishes *art* from *tools*, thus indicating that within the class of man-made things we want to make further distinctions.

One attempt at narrowing the class, and I believe one of the first steps in the development of institutional theories of art, was that of Urmson, who suggested that art be defined as an "artifact primarily intended for aesthetic consideration."[12] The ambiguities which weaken Dickie's definition, the failure to specify what the "artworld" is and what being presented as "a candidate for appreciation" entails (see chapter 2, section vii), reappear here in the phrase "primarily intended for aesthetic consideration."

Behind these attempts to limit the class of all artifacts is the open-minded attitude forced upon us by contemporary art, though it is not strictly confined to our century. The presence of soup cans and urinals in our museums seems to preclude anything but an affirmative answer to the question, "You mean all you have to do to make something a work of art is to *say* that it is a work of art?" Remarks like this one of Brunius illustrate that this attitude is not confined to a hostile, uninformed public:

> Art happens to be a big cage in which different birds fly in and out. At any time items are selected, serving as paradigms. What resembles these paradigms is considered art. So "art" is not at all a class of items with a common property. It is a bundle of quite different items, activities as well

as objects, and what makes them art is that persons are pointing at them saying that they are works of art. [13]

If this were true, that one could make a thing a work of art just by saying so, it would make the class of works of art very special (as well as very large). One cannot make just anything a horse or a virus or an ashtray or a true statement or a benevolent action simply by pointing and saying, "That's a horse," "That's an ashtray," or "That's true." Of course we sometimes have difficulties deciding whether a particular thing before us actually is a horse, a virus, an ashtray, a true statement, or a benevolent action. Often we must look at a theory and its paradigms in order to settle the matter. But if one points at a horse and says, "That's an ashtray," the mere pointing and saying will convince no one. Why, then, are we convinced when someone merely points and says, "That's a work of art"?

The answer is that we—or at least many of us—are not; indeed, as I've already suggested in chapter 1, this is a very unsatisfactory situation. It must be possible to narrow the class of artifacts so that they are not all automatically works of art. The second condition in my definition, then—namely, that the artifact be discussed in such a way that "information concerning its history of production directs the viewer's attention to properties which are worth attending to"—is meant to solve precisely this problem.

Even radical theorists, those who appear to think that simply saying an object is a work of art is enough to make it one, ultimately must insist that the right persons do the saying. Picking out the legitimate pointers is what Danto and Dickie are getting at in their use of the term 'artworld'. It is members of social, cultural, political, and economic institutions like museums that belong to this artworld and have, apparently, the necessary credentials for naming something a work of art.

But the artworld does not consist solely of pointers and dubbers. The pointers and dubbers must be prepared to describe and discuss in certain ways the things they point to and dub. And it is at this point that the notion of critical exposure becomes central. We have seen that critics, historians, and theorists give us "recommendations of how we should experience works of art," [14] and that they do this by providing us with information about history of production that focuses our attention on certain properties of the objects in question. I have explained already what I mean by 'history of production', but have not explained what I mean by 'properties worth attending to'; and the addition of this phrase will, of course, be useless unless it can be clarified. As it stands, the phrase is as (if not more) ambiguous and vague as "primarily intended for aesthetic consideration."

The first thing which must be true of these properties is that they be *intrinsic*. This is a term that I have used (along with 'extrinsic') quite often thus far in the discussion. I have argued that in discussing works of art, reference to properties "outside" of the work as well as "inside" it can be relevant. I now wish to elaborate what I proposed at the outset of this chapter: that what makes reference to extrinsic properties, in particular those having to do with a work's history of production, relevant is that this reference directs attention to intrinsic properties.

By 'intrinsic' I mean something quite simple—namely, 'perceivable'. Ideally, one would hope that a nondispositional term could be found to describe the nature of these properties, but I think this is impossible; for works of art typically cannot be "gotten" all at once. We've seen that features of a work often are not accessible except to persons who have special training. One cannot perceive that a piece is written in a minor key unless one has been trained to distinguish minor from major keys. One who does not know what metopes are will not notice that Ionic temples lack them.

Or works have too much to be taken in all at once. As Kenneth Clark has said, "I fancy that one cannot enjoy a pure aesthetic sensation (so-called) for longer than one can enjoy the smell of an orange, which in my case is less than two minutes; but one must look attentively at a great work of art for longer than that, and the value of historical criticism is that it keeps the attention fixed on the work while the senses have time to get a second wind."[15] What is essential is that there be properties that *can* be perceived directly. I am painfully aware of how difficult the notion of being 'directly perceivable' is. We must, for example, allow the use of instruments such as eye glasses. Clark emphasizes the role of the senses, though often, as in reading literature, it is as much a matter of cognition as sensation; sometimes we must use our imaginations to "see" what an object must have been like once (see Plate I).

> In its present state, the *Medusa* is a partial ruin. Bituminous paints, which Géricault used to deepen the shadows, have dulled its surface and darkened its colour, The first impression it gives is one of brownish darkness, shot through with lighter patches of yellowish or greenish hue. Yet the picture does not lack colour. The actual richness which makes up its sombre harmony becomes apparent only when the eye has adjusted to the abrupt play of light and shadow, and has learned to make allowance for the damage which the decaying bitumen has produced in its surface.[16]

Further, we must, often grudgingly, admit that some persons possess keener senses and that probably some features of objects are beyond the perception of the majority of the population. In his essay "Of a Standard of Taste,"[17] Hume retells a Sancho Panza story about two men, highy reputed winetasters, who criticize the wine at a festival as being good but having, first, a slight metallic and, second, a slight leathery taste. The rest of the drinkers believe, deep down, that the two are just pretending to taste metal and leather in order to maintain their reputations. But when the last of the wine is drained from the barrel, other drinkers discover a metal key on a leather thong. That some people have "better taste," or a "finer ear" (whether it be a matter totally of training or partly an inborn facility), must be admitted. However, works of art must possess properties which in principle can be perceived—and in practice we require that at least more than one person can perceive them in a work.

The phrase 'in the work' here is very important. Notice the difference in the following descriptions written by Washington Irving. (See plate IV.) The first relates a local story told by the guide, Mateo; the second describes a court-yard.

There was once an invalid soldier, who had charge of the Alhambra to show it to strangers; as he was one evening, about twilight, passing through the court of Lions, he heard footsteps on the Hall of the Albencerrages; suppos-ing some strangers to be lingering there, he advanced to attend upon them, when to his astonishment he beheld four Moors richly dressed, with gilded cuirasses and cimeters, and poinards glittering with precious stones. They were walking to and fro with solemn pace; but paused and beckoned to him. The old soldier, however, took flight, and could never afterwards be pre-vailed upon to enter the Alhambra. Thus it is that men sometimes turn their backs upon fortune; for it is the firm opinion of Mateo, that the Moors intended to reveal the place where their treasures lay buried. A successor to the invalid soldier was more knowing; he came to the Alhambra poor; but at the end of a year went off to Malaga, bought houses, set up a carriage, and still lives there, one of the richest as well as oldest men of the place, all which, Mateo sagely surmised, was in consequence of finding out the golden secret of these phantom Moors.[18]

Passing from the court of the Alberca under a Moorish archway we enter the renowned court of Lions. No part of this edifice gives a more complete idea of its original beauty than this, for none has suffered so little from the ravages of time. In the centre stands the fountain famous in song and story. The alabaster basins still shed the diamond drops; the twelve lions which support them, and give the court its name, still cast forth crystal streams as in the days of Boabdil. The lions, however, are unworthy of their fame, being of miserable sculpture, the work probably of some Christian cap-tive.[19]

Probably both of these passages add to the visitor's overall apreciation of the complex. But only the second refers to intrinsic properties. "Books have to be read (worse luck for it takes a long time); it is the only way of discovering what they contain,"[20] jokes E. M. Forster. Intrinsic properties are those which one cannot perceive without reading the book—or doing whatever is required to perceive a particular art form.

Looking back to chapter 2, then, we see that what makes reference to extrinsic qualities important and relevant is that they direct our attention to the work (indeed, this is what critics suspicious of personal or historical or Freudian approaches want to require). Some references may divert attention— a viewer may be more interested in the king's attitude toward El Greco's paintings than to the paintings themselves. But most critical discussion is intended to have the opposite effect. Historians and critics may themselves get so caught up in a fact about the artist's life or culture that the work takes a back seat. But I think the examples of chapter 2 do, when we read them, cause us to look *at the work* with increasing attention and renewed interest.

We can see again here how all this really depends on the first condition of the definition: that is, for all this attention to a work's internal properties to be possible, the work must be an accessible artifact. Naming properties that are worth attending to demands that we be able to perceive the things named. If works of art were completely "fleeting," we couldn't be brought to perceive anything that we missed first time round. If a work is destroyed, then the perception or conception is not possible. Identity of sensations and ideas is by no means an easy notion. But if Housman had not written the line "Sprinkle the quarters on the morning town," and if the line had not been preserved, there certainly would have been fewer perceptions and conceptions in the world. It is wrong to say, "Oh, we might have had the same sensations and ideas caused by something else." If a viewer responds affirmatively when asked, "Do you see the balance now?" there is no way of proving that he or she is telling the truth. But we can be sure that the balance will *not* be seen again if the work is destroyed.

Thus the properties worth attending to are intrinsic and directly perceivable. It is not possible to give a complete list of what an object's directly perceivable qualities are. Of course, what I have in mind are things such as size, color, weight, sound, shape, number of syllables, key, rhythmic pattern, and texture. But not all of these are always (say the number of syllables) or even usually (weight, for instance), important. The thinness of stone is crucial to an appreciation of Thorvaldsen's *Christ* (see figure 13) but not to the Court of Lions (see plate IV). Exactly which intrinsic properties are "worth attending to"?

The immediate response one tends to give to such a question is, "Why, the aesthetic ones, of course." But the problem of distinguishing aesthetic and nonaesthetic properties is notoriously difficult; if it had been solved the problem of distinguishing art from nonart would be much easier.[21]

Sometimes someone calls to me, "Come look at the sunset!" I don't have to ask "Why?" for it is generally agreed that sunsets have properties (specifically colors and their combinations) that are worth attending to—properties which provide us with some satisfaction. There are artifacts which are like this too; we don't have to convince others that they bear attention, it being generally understood that they are things that people are glad to perceive. Although there is no general formula for what those things are in which we find satisfaction, we can enumerate some of them. They are things which delight our senses, delight our intellect, educate us, provide an escape from the tedium of everyday life, excite us, enrich our experience, amuse us, stimulate our imaginations, enhance communication.

The phrase "worth attending to" basically refers to the things people mention when they give us reasons in support of the claim that the thing they are talking about will give us satisfaction; and these things may differ from culture to culture, period to period. It includes formal as well as affective and abstract intellectual properties. The special ways which art historians, critics, and theorists have of describing things create traditions (I prefer this term to 'institutions') in which certain things are taken to be worth attending to. It is part of our culture that we admire sunsets. Similarly, it is part of our culture (probably all cultures) to admire artifacts which delight our senses and our intellects. Schools or traditions of criticism and history emphasize various properties which are believed to give rise to such delight. Artifacts are valued because they are harmonious, balanced, rhythmic, expressive, or vivid. We are told to "notice the relation of shapes" because the tradition of criticism holds that relationship to be worth perceiving.

This explains both why we have to be taught to perceive certain properties and why different objects receive different aesthetic evaluations in different periods of history. Traditions change, and what that means is that new or different properties are considered worth attending to. Those unfamiliar with the traditions not only have to be convinced that they will be glad to perceive some property, they have to be brought to perceive it in the first place. Changes in the history of an art form are accompanied by changes in the descriptions of theorists and critics. Different properties will be considered more or less important in different periods, for instance, at one time color will be considered more important than line and then line will come to dominate. Or plot will be considered all important in one period, characterization in another.

Or terms disappear. Luis Barragán, who received the 1980 Pritzker Architecture Prize, declared at the award ceremony that "an alarming proportion of publications devoted to architecture have banished from their pages the words beauty, inspiration, magic, spellbound, enchantment. . . ."[22] The most general, historically speaking, of all aesthetic terms, 'beauty', has, as Jerome Stolnitz says, "receded or even disappeared from contemporary aesthetic theory."[23] It has moved from the central position in aesthetic evaluation to a more peripheral position, with 'aesthetic' taking on the central role. As art and artists have become less and less concerned with giving us something beautiful (preferring the expressive or the interesting), the term has undergone what Stolnitz calls a "transvaluation." It is very nearly considered a weakness on the part of an artist to provide something that is "only beautiful." Stolnitz believes that the demotion of beauty began with eighteenth-century failures to discover an objective basis for judgments about the beauty of a thing. Whether or not this is the whole story, when *beauty* was at the core, some other properties were considered more worthy of attending to than they are now: *neat, trim, delicate, polished, proportioned, refined*, have been supplanted by *engaging, gripping, disturbing, exciting, ambiguous, innovative*. That the pendulum may have begun its sweep back is perhaps signaled by Douglas Davis's assessment that "the current revulsion from modernist architecture suggests that the public wants more than functional content. Barragán's special task has been to satisfy some of these forgotten psychic needs—for beauty, magic and silence. Finally, that task has received a just and fitting tribute." [24] The activity of art history (at least as it seems to be understood by Gombrich) is largely aimed at the discovery of the predominant properties in periods and styles different from our own and at tracing such changes of theoretical emphasis.

P. F. Strawson predicts that a method such as I am proposing, "an examination of the kinds of language we typically use in articulating assessments of the kind concerned," will get bogged down in the "limitless elasticity and variety of the vocabulary of criticism. . . ."[25] Certainly the vocabulary art critics and historians use is very wide and seemingly endless. But the same terms do crop up again and again, and therein lies the key to understanding the special treatment we give to works of art. Essentially, I propose that we identify aesthetic discussions and proceed to see what properties they emphasize, on the assumption that it is these properties which are considered worth attending to.

How do we tell which discussions are aesthetic? If such identification is done in terms of 'works of art'—for example, "Aesthetic discussions are those surrounding works of art"— then my definition falters, for clearly we are using the very term 'work of art' to define 'work of art'. We might strengthen the definition by relying on works of art considered paradigmatic, but it would be preferable to depend on some other concept entirely.

We have to begin by relying on our intuitions to some extent. But perhaps we can do it in a less viciously circular way. Let us identify aesthetic discussions by using a term other than 'work of art', one that we all agree is an aesthetic term. I referred earlier to the fact that 'beauty' has moved from its place at the center of aesthetics and that related terms such as 'neat', 'delicate', and 'trim' have accompanied 'beauty' on the trip from center. A history of the use of 'beauty' and of its move from center would, I believe, be illuminating; but because of the immensity of the task it probably could not be adequately completed. However, a history of some other term might be conducted; indeed I believe a recent one provides exactly the sort of case study we need.

The work I have in mind is Walter Cahn's *Masterpieces*, and the term is 'masterpiece' itself. Like 'beauty', 'masterpiece' is one that we all can agree is a general aesthetic term. It has its metaphoric uses (we can praise razor blades or lightbulbs as "masterpieces of technology") but its core use is to describe things we all identify as works of art—novels, symphonies, statues, and so on. Unlike 'beauty', which has always been an aesthetic term, 'masterpiece' has the, for us, added advantage of not always having been one. By tracing the shift in function from one primarily nonaesthetic to one primarily aesthetic, we can locate corresponding shifts in associated properties. Just being told that something is a masterpiece does not do much in the way of drawing attention to its intrinsic properties. But in the contexts in which it appears we find reference to more specific properties. In its original, nonaesthetic, use, things were pointed to that are no longer pointed to. These have been supplanted by a different set of properties and these can be identified as aesthetic properties.

It is beyond the scope of this book to do more than suggest how this method of distinguishing aesthetic from nonaesthetic properties works, or to discuss fully Cahn's work. Cahn explains the original use of 'masterpiece', "to designate the project assigned to an apprentice or journeyman as a qualifying trial required for acceptance into a professional guild."[26] This is a far cry from our notion of a masterpiece as the culminating accomplishment of an artist's lifework. The artisanal tasks, often having specific time requirements, were assigned to butchers, tailors, and locksmiths, as well as sculptors (stonecutters) and painters. The appearance of terms such as 'proportion' or 'marvelous' in discussions of masterpieces waited upon its development as an aesthetic term, as did the disappearance of "completed in three months" or "knowledgeable enough in this operation." By thus studying the history of a central term, I believe we can come to identify "properties considered worth attending to" within historical and critical traditions.

We need, perhaps, to clarify certain other things about the second part of my definition. The second condition stipulates that "x is discussed. . . ." The 'is' here is intended to be timeless in the sense that it can be interpreted as having a past and future as well as a present state of being. An object which used to be discussed in such a way, but is no longer, has ceased to be a work of art. (I believe, as a matter of fact, that this rarely happens. The change which takes place in the class of things which are works of art is more one of growth than shift.) Similarly, an object which has not yet been discussed in the requisite way may be discussed later and will then become an art work. Just as we may say, "Has that always been an ashtray?" "No, it used to be a pie tin," so we can say, "Has that always been a work of art?" " No, it used to be a pie tin." And even: "Has that always been an ashtray?" "No, it used to be a work of art." I have already argued that even natural objects like pieces of driftwood or lava take on the status of artifacts by being treated as if they were products of human rather than natural activity. Similarly here, it is the way that objects are treated that makes the crucial difference.

When we identify an object as an ashtray rather than as a pie tin, it is because we choose different features as the relevant ones. Nelson Goodman argues in his essay "When is Art?" that art can be understood in part by analogy with tailors' swatches.[27] (He also discusses this analogy in his *Languages of Art*.) Pieces of cloth that function as samples of the bolt from which they come do so only when a system of symbolizing or exemplifying exists which allows us to know what properties the swatches are known to represent. Our experiences with tailors and upholsterers teaches us that the small pieces we are shown exemplify some, but not all, of the properties of the bolt—color but not size, for instance. Likewise, objects can function as art only when they operate within a system in which only some of their own properties are relevant to their interpretation as art works—for example, color, but not proximity to a museum's restrooms.

Of course the properties critics within a particular tradition consider important will not necessarily be properties which people unfamiliar with the tradition will be able to perceive immediately. We have already noted that we sometimes have to learn a specialized vocabulary ('metope', 'hyperbole', 'augmented fifth', 'inscape'). But we must also admit that even familiar terms often give us difficulty—and consulting a dictionary may not really help. "The composition is spatially balanced" is an opaque statement to someone who does not quite know what to look for. Often readers conclude, as did the common drinkers at Sancho Panza's party, that critics utter only empty phrases in order to maintain their lofty reputations. Sometimes, of course, this conclusion is justified. But it also frequently demonstrates that the reader does not fully share with the critic basic assumptions, vocabulary, and beliefs. As Rudolf Arnheim shows in his *Art and Visual Perception*, terms like 'balance', 'shape', 'form', 'space', 'light', 'color', 'movement', 'tension', and 'expression' are only *apparently* simple and straightforward. A description of Cézanne's portrait of his wife as a "balanced composition" leaves an outsider cold. Arnheim's analysis of the balancing forces in this painting comes at the end of a complex chapter in which he explains balance, thus showing that some knowledge of psychology and physics, knowing what and how we see, is required before we can fully appreciate what critics and historians have been pointing to when they refer to art objects.[28]

Consider again Rosenthal and Smith's comment on Housman's poem *Eight O'Clock* at the beginning of chapter 2. The poem and the comments are straightforward—clearer than most poetry and criticism. But a reader who does not know what feet and beats are will be lost. And learning to interpret an object correctly entails, as we have seen, more than simply learning a new vocabulary. As Jack Hobbs says, "We should . . . be sensitive to the fact that a Peruvian shepherd or an Alaskan Indian may find an American comic strip as incomprehensible as he would find our game of football. To know nothing about the anxieties of growing up in suburban America, public schools, summer camps, and peer relationships is to virtually eliminate the whole content of *Peanuts*. But before a Peruvian shepherd could even get to this point, he would still have to make sense out of the little lines and shapes drawn on the paper. The lesson is not that one group of people is more sophisticated or more primitive than another, but that each group develops different ways of seeing and behaving. One's environment and past experiences affect the way one sees things, and the *way* that one sees, in turn, affects much of *what* one sees. Any discussion of meaning and style in art should start with this as a base. The student who desires to discover more in art must be willing to make an effort to go beyond his own present habits of looking at art."[29] This is what critics help us to do.

The reason that *influence* is so often emphasized in discussions of artists and their work is that it provides a means of identifying the tradition in terms of which a work is to be discussed. Comparison of one work with another centers attention on the properties such a tradition stresses. One of the problems with contemporary art (and the reason that the orange-crate and moose-call examples make any sense at all) is that the audience does not know what properties are supposed to be looked at and/or how they are to be related to one another. Viewing individual artifacts without any idea about what one should look for is apt to be meaningless and frustrating.

Thus the definition

x is a work of art if and only if (1) x is an artifact and (2) x is discussed in such a way that information concerning the history of production of x will direct the viewer's attention to properties which are worth attending to cannot stand in isolation, that is, independent of history or traditions of art and criticism. But if 'work of art' is defined in terms of 'properties worth attending to' and if 'properties worth attending to' are those properties identified as important in discussions of works of art, don't we have a vicious circularity? Does it follow from the definition that if nothing had been identified as a work of art, and if those things had not been discussed, we could not distinguish art from nonart? The answer is "yes." A particular object cannot be identified as art independent of the traditions of art, art history, art criticism, and art theory. To expect this is unreasonable. It would be like trying to prove that doing one's duty is moral independently of all previous moral discussion; or it would be like deciding whether the liquid we are drinking is wine without referring to any concepts previously used in discussing wines. "We're going to consider a whole new concept of wine now." Surely without being told a great deal more, this is impossible.

Even abstract or conceptual art doesn't completely begin again, even though its practitioners sometimes say that they have developed a "new concept" of art. Certain features of the earlier traditions are still necessary—the object is to be looked at, just as our new wine will have to be tasted. And certainly a "new" artistic approach is somehow a reaction to the old ones. My definition will admittedly be of no help to people who have no conception of what art is or of the way people have talked about it. I would be very surprised if it did.

It might be objected that this definition of 'art' places undue emphasis on talking about it. Couldn't there have been works of art if there had been no critics, historians, or theorists of art? This question is misleading. In one sense, there certainly could have been objects produced by people utterly unconcerned about how other people would describe them. My claim is that the term 'work of art', used to identify a subclass of artifacts, requires the special kind of describing found in citicism and history. Does this mean that history and criticism are more important than creation? No—no claim about importance is being made at all. A feature of an organism may not be the most important or interesting thing about it, but nevertheless may serve to distinguish it from all other organisms.

The real test of the definition comes in seeing whether it does allow us to say now of a particular object that it is or is not a work of art. Which artifacts in the rooms in which we find ourselves are discussed in ways that lead us to attend more closely to intrinsic properties worth attending to if we are told something about their history of production? Notice that the theory does not just say that knowing something about an artifact's history of production will make us look more closely at an object. Rather, being given specific information will direct our attention to specific intrinsic properties identified as worth attending to by traditions of criticism and history. If we are told that one author knows more about young women than another, we look more closely at the particular descriptions each gives us. If we are told an artist chose to portray that moment when a steamer turned away from the life raft, we look more closely at the little ship in the background. If we are told that a painting was created in the eighteenth century, and if we know something about the eighteenth century, we look for signs of the enlightenment attitude toward the world. Usually, the more specific the information we are given, the more help we get in seeing what we are supposed to see. Knowledge concerning an object's history of production may be very complicated or very simple. But at the very least we must know that it is an artifact before it can be appreciated as a work of art. And whatever the particular information about the reference to history of production is, it must direct our attention to an intrinsic property which, within a particular tradition, is identified as "aesthetic."

"This was the first bottle ever made to contain Coca-Cola." (See plate V.) If we are told that about an object before us on the table, chances are we will look at the bottle more carefully. We will attend to the shape, color, and texture of glass more carefully, and surely these are paradigms of what we think of as aesthetic properties. Does it follow then that the coke bottle is a work of art?

For a time I was bothered by such examples, for I strongly feel that not everything is a work of art; and if we let in Coke bottles, how can we fairly keep anything out? Jasper Johns's bronze Ballantine beer cans are not so troubling, for they are not real beer bottles. They are not used to hold beer, do not sit neglected in the refrigerator, do not attract ants in the garage, do not litter our highways. And they are, after all, bronze. All of these facts allow at least superficial differentiation and provide a way for maintaining some standards and/or prejudices. But what we have here is an honest-to-goodness Coke bottle, not to be distinguished from hundreds of others just like it, except by its date of production.

What has comforted me, finally, is the presence of objects like a blue bottle, part of a Pompeii exhibition offered at Louisiana Museum in Denmark in the fall of 1977. Except for the fact that the bottle was uncovered at a certain spot in Pompeii, very little is known about it. Was it a decoration, or part of the everyday furnishings of someone's home or restaurant? Let us suppose that it was included in the exhibit not simply because it survived the holocaust and is interesting historically (which is certainly a large part of the reason for its inclusion) but also because it has a pretty color and a nice shape. Can our Coke bottle be blackballed because it lacks these properties? No. It does have a rather nice shape and color.

It is simply not possible to draw a sharp line between things which are art and things which are not. To continue the metaphor of the exclusive club, it is as if some things are given associate, but not full membership. Ordinarily, knowledge concerning the history of production of pop bottles does not cause us to look at them differently than we did before. We find bottling plants fascinating. Machines which dispense just the right amount of colored liquid into containers which are propelled by another machine to have labels stuck upon them by steel hands have a compelling attraction. Usually we do not look any more closely at one of those bottles the next time we drink from it. However, we might. Coke bottles can be observed as if they were works of art. Aesthetic properties of Coke bottles—properties worth attending to—are often neglected. They are not presented in contexts where it is customary to point to them. Knowing its history of production, particularly in cases like the one in which we are told, "This is the first one ever made," can have the effect of our being asked to look at it and talk about it as if it were a work of art.

One difference between the blue bottle from Pompeii and the Coke bottle is that we now view the Pompeian bottle *only* in contexts where we realize that we are supposed to treat it in certain ways, as an aesthetic object. Fill it with water and place it on a restaurant table and its shape and color may also be overlooked. This is, of course, the important lesson that much of twentieth-century art has taught us.

I have often wondered how many little boys have been relieved to see Rauschenberg's urinal, only to be disappointed when told, "No, *not* there." Not everyone sees the urinal as a work of art. But when enough people do, it becomes one. The important thing here is not to try to decide what the precise point is when an object or event becomes a work of art, but to realize that being seen as a work entails that we discuss it in certain ways, and look at it in certain ways, upon learning something about its history of production. Why are football games not works of art? Because they are not discussed *mainly* in aesthetic terms. They could be, and if they were, they would become works of art.

Suppose a geologist looks at a mountain. Knowing the "history of production" of the mountain will very probably make him or her notice things about a chunk of rock taken from it that the average viewer overlooks. For example, in addition to noticing the pale pink color running through the stone, the geologist will notice the angle it makes with other-colored folded layers of minerals. In this case we are "saved" from being forced to call the rock a work of art because it is not an artifact. But suppose a sculptor carves a statue from it, intentionally retaining the pink and other layers. Notice that there is a difference between looking at the stone as a stone and looking at it as a statue. Knowing that the rock has the properties it has as a result of natural forces is not aesthetically relevant—although knowing that the artist carefully chose this piece of rock because of its special colors is. The pressure rocks have undergone for millions of years is not the sort of thing we normally hear referred to in discussions of sculpture, though perhaps it may be one day.

To repeat, it is not simply that knowing the history of production makes a thing more interesting to us. Suppose that while viewing a dam we are told that seven men lost their lives in its construction. The fact that this is the sort of statistic often reported (and often exaggerated) in connection with such structures indicates that it is the sort of thing which increases or enriches the onlookers' interest. Like the guide's story as related by Washington Irving, it enriches the experience, but does not call attention to intrinsic properties which are generally held to be worth attending to.

But (apologizing for ghoulishness) one might object that someone could say, "And look, you can see a foot sticking out of the concrete over there." Hasn't attention now been called to an intrinsic property of the dam generally (by the majority of the public) held to be worth attending to? Yes—but not to an intrinsic property generally considered worth attending to in discussions of art objects, within any important critical or artistic tradition.

In addition to the traditions of criticism which determine, and to some extent delimit, what counts as works of art, there are two other related factors that contribute to distinguishing the class of art objects from the class of all objects. Perhaps the most famous essay dealing with what most people would consider a nonartistic artifact is Henry Adams's "The Dynamo and the Virgin." In it Adams refers to intrinsic as well as extrinsic properties. He explains:

> [T]o Adams the dynamo became a symbol of infinity. As he grew accustomed to the great gallery of machines, be began to feel the forty-foot dynamo as a moral force, much as the early Christians felt the cross. The planet itself seemed less impressive, in its old-fashioned, deliberate, annual or daily revolution, than this huge wheel, revolving within arm's-length at some vertiginous speed, and barely murmuring—scarcely humming an audible warning to stand a hair's breadth further for respect of power—while it would not wake the baby lying close against its frame.[30]

Certainly machines as well as churches or paintings inspired by the Virgin have properties worth attending to. But what Nelson Goodman refers to as "repleteness"[31] is relevant to paintings and architecture in a way that it is not to the dynamo. 'Repleteness' is a relative term referring to the fact that in some objects, properties are considered constitutive that are considered contingent in other objects. For example, the color of ink used in a seismograph is not important to the record made, that is, color is contingent to our reading the score of an earth tremor on the Richter scale. However, the color of ink in a drawing is not a contingent matter, not irrelevant to the interests we have in it. Drawings, then, are more replete with respect to color than are seismograms. The importance which Adams justifiably grants to the dynamo does not depend, for example, upon the screws being just where they are and nowhere else, in the way that the importance of Virgin paintings does depend upon, for example, the brushstrokes being just where they are. Perhaps some dynamos are viewed primarily for their design, and then the precise location of the screws might become important. 'Design' is not totally removed from the area of 'art', but it should be remembered that there is a difference between enjoying design and enjoying design after realizing that it has a particular history of production.

An additional thing that is special about works of art, and one that I have alluded to above, is the fact that we want to keep them safe. We have obligations to preserve works of art so that others may perceive them after us. Alan Tormey has provided a very neat argument for the existence of aesthetic rights (and hence obligations). An entity has rights, he presupposes, if it possesses interests that generate obligations. Tormey shows that artworks do possess such interests by examining what he calls "aesthetic pain." Aesthetic pains (for example hearing music played off-key or seeing clumsily performed dances or dramatic productions) are caused, at least in some instances, by our recognition of a distortion in or incongruity between a performance and a work. They result when we recognize that a work has been done some violence or injustice. Thus we, at least sometimes, recognize that things can be or have been done to works of art that are objectionable: they can be marred, distorted, debased, done violence to, affronted—they can be *mistreated*. It follows directly from this that we regard art works as possessing interests that are obligation generating; we expect people to fulfill certain obligations with respect to them.[32]

We may briefly admire the color and shape of a coke bottle, but we feel no compunction about returning it for the deposit. Or, if it breaks, we do not feel a sense of irreplaceable loss. There are thousands of other bottles which we feel sure will afford us the same satisfaction. We believe, on the other hand, that only Géricault's *Raft of the Medusa* will give rise to certain experiences (sensations and ideas) and hence we insist that there is a crucial difference between it and reproductions of it.[33] Furthermore, although we may feel obligated to preserve the dynamo, the obligation is not the obligation to preserve it *simply in order that others may perceive it*. If we preserve and protect objects (historical sites, for example) just so that others may benefit from the mere perception of them, then those objects do begin to take on the status of works of art.

In chapter 3, I claimed that distinguishing art from nonart is not merely an idle philosophic exercise. There are, as we saw in the case of the Hartford boulders, genuine practical matters involved. How then can this proposed definition of 'work of art' be of use in such situations?

The Andre sculpture was financed by the Hartford Foundation for Public Giving and by federal funds through the National Endowment for the Arts. Public funds are more and more widely used to support the arts, and in most cases committees must select artist recipients from a pool of many applicants. A recent newspaper article reported that

> more than a billion dollars a year now go to U.S. cultural grants, and a billion dollars means hard competition. The federal arts and humanities endowments alone directly invest about $215 million. Cultural grants show up in the budgets of other agencies, from the Fulbright scholarships to the job programs for artists of the Department of Health, Education, and Welfare. State and local governments contribute considerable amounts independently and on a matching basis. Corporate cultural grants alone were estimated last year to be $211 million, much of it matching the government and the foundations.[34]

Public funds appropriated for "the arts" must be used as such. Hence it is essential that there be a working definition, both in order that committees can give grants for suitable activity and in order that the public can determine whether funds raised through taxation are being used appropriately, if not wisely and well.

Suppose a funding committee is confronted with the following proposals:

1. "I'm going to put an orange crate in a grassy area and put crab grass in it."

2. "I'm going to wipe my paint brushes on my garage door."

3. "I'm going to bake a gigantic wedding cake and eat it."

4. "I'm going to bake a gigantic wedding cake and paint it red."

5. "I'm going to bake a gigantic wedding cake and put it next to the Eternal Flame under the Arc de Triomphe."

6. "I'm going to run a fence through Minnesota."

All of these can be looked at "aesthetically," that is, can be viewed in terms of properties which are part of traditional aesthetic discussions—color, shape, gracefulness, expressiveness, and so on. But, as they stand, none of these proposals will result in things which will automatically be viewed aesthetically by the public. If the committee is to choose wisely, it must be given more information; the applicants will need to explain just how what they intend to do will result in a work of art. The committee must determine if any of the proposals really involve the creation of works of art. This can be done, I believe, by asking whether there will be produced an artifact which will be discussed in such a way that information concerning its history of production will lead viewers to focus on properties traditionally considered worth attending to. This happened in the case of Andre's "Stone Field Sculpture" when viewers learned that he chose boulders from an area near Hartford, that several of the stones were the same type as those used in many Hartford buildings, that the artist had visited and been impressed by Stonehenge, that he intended that the space be seen as a whole, with the stones as indentations, and so on. [35]

Ask yourself what, if anything, would lead you to accept any of the six proposals above as involving real works of art. In order to be acceptable, each must, I believe, include reference to information concerning history of production which brings the perceiver to concentrate on traditional aesthetic properties. In the six cases above, readers should try to imagine how critical discussions might proceed in order to convince us that we have a genuine art work.

Could someone try to make a work of art and fail? Since anything can be looked at "aesthetically," for everything has at least shape and color, how can we ever say that someone who has made the attempt to produce a work of art has not succeeded? Of course, someone could fail to produce an artifact and hence fail under the first condition. The lack of a notation or documentation accounts for the fact that merely eating a piece of cake now is not a work of art, no matter how gracefully it is done. As we saw earlier in this chapter, accessibility and repeatability must in principle be possible.

But is it possible, given that one succeeds in producing an accessible artifact, to try to create a work of art and fail? Here all we can rely on is the presence or absence of aesthetic properties identified as such through the traditional means and emphasized by information concerning history of production. Not everything with color or shape is discussed in such a way that such information will draw attention to these properties. Nor does the mere fact that something is treated in a special way (for example, a coke bottle is placed on a mantel) ensure that it will be talked about in a special way.

Suppose my son walks across the freshly mopped kitchen floor wearing boots, leaving a pattern of chunks of dirt. Knowing my toleration for 'works of art' he may try to excuse himself by saying, "But Mom, I made a work of art." How can I avoid being taken in? I can simply insist that no tradition exists that allows either for suitable repetition of the action or for discussion of it. Failure here follows from the fact that nothing about the history of production calls attention to properties of the pattern of dirt in any clear or traditional way. If my son is a recognized abstract expressionist, on the other hand, my scolding is on shakier grounds. Intending to create a work of art amounts to intending to create an artifact that will be discussed within a tradition of history, theory, and criticism. Clearly the intention to create something that will be talked about in a special way is one that can fail to be fulfilled.

My response to the pattern of mud on the kitchen floor is probably not much different from the response of many people visiting museums in which the objects displayed come from traditions with which they are unfamiliar (see again figure 1), or of people who go to concerts where what is performed is untraditional. Since not all people living today are acquainted with the traditions of the modern artworld, such experiences are often confusing. Often, I think, the claim that something is "nonart" is a moral or evaluative claim. People feel that they are being deceived or not treated seriously. Or they believe that the patterns of paint or sound they see or hear do not amount to something "pleasing" or "profound" or "expressive." But there are certainly times when a descriptive claim is being made. How can people decide whether or not these (perhaps bad or immoral) objects or events are, descriptively, art?

I believe that most people who learn something about the history of production of the objects and performances confronting them are brought to admit that these things deserve to be called "art." Their confusion results from a lack of familiarity with developing aesthetic traditions. This is, of course, an empirical claim not unlike Hume's claim that everyone who has read both Ogilby and Milton prefers Milton.[36] However, I am not at all bothered by the possible use of empirical tests for my theory.

Finally, in defense of this definition of 'work of art', I must point out that it averts two of the dangers that Morris Weitz believes all such definitions necessarily fall prey to. First, it does not turn an open concept into a closed one. As we saw in chapter 1, Weitz claims that the "very expansive, adventurous character of art" puts it beyond definition.[38] To the extent that traditions of art, criticism, history, and theory develop and change, to that extent this definition allows for development and change. Part of artists' creativity consists in broadening the class of properties considered worth attending to, though never changing that class all at once.

Second, this definition does not deprive 'work of art' of its function as both a descriptive and evaluative term. At one and the same time 'work of art' picks out members of a class and assigns a value to those things. We have in this chapter been concerned with the descriptive function: How do we know which of the things in the room are artworks? We can turn now to the question: How do we tell the good works of art from the bad ones?

5
Good and Bad Works of Art

One of the most serious objections to the theory I have proposed is this: If an object has properties worth attending to, must it not necessarily follow that the object thereby has a positive value? If my theory is correct, it seems to follow that bad works of art do not exist. Those who believe that the term 'work of art' is always honorific, comparable, say, to 'saint', will not raise this objection. But not everyone, myself included, believes the term functions this way.

It is generally held that judging something to be 'good' amounts to judging it as 'good of its kind'. Thus the claim that something is "a good knife" is possible only if we have already determined that it is a knife. 'x is a good knife' implies 'x is a knife'. Now suppose that from a proposed definition of 'knife', it followed that 'x is a bad knife' implied 'x is not a knife'. We would then obviously be faced with a contradiction.

Similarly, if saying that something is a work of art always entails assigning positive value to that thing, then the determination that a thing has negative (or no positive) value would be tantamount to determining that it is not a work of art. But one of the functions of criticism is evaluation, and it is absurd to claim that when critics evaluate an object negatively they are not engaged in the same kind of activity as when they evaluate something in positive terms. Consider, for instance, Ballo's comparison of Jean Fouquet's *Portrait of Charles VII of France* (fourteenth century, Louvre) with an eighteenth-century portrait by an unknown artist of Joseph II of Austria.

> Fouquet, a great painter, did not consider his sitter merely as a pretext, but endowed a large composition with a stringent rhythm, based on austere draughtsmanship harmonizing with subtle color values. The other portrait, of Joseph II of Austria . . . is nothing more than an illustration, executed with meticulous care. It has no rhythm, the sitter's attitude is casual and it is lifeless; it is just an ordinary photograph (like a modern passport photo) and in no sense is it a work of art.[1]

124

Ballo's critical theory, greatly simplified, is that works of art have "rhythm," and since rhythm is a positive, good-making property, it follows that works of art that possess it are good. But when he claims that the portrait of Joseph II is "in no sense . . . a work of art" he must be speaking evaluatively. If the portrait were not literally, or in what Weitz calls the descriptive sense, a work of art, then it surely would be meaningless, or at least unfair, to compare it to something that is. Like 'rhythm', my 'properties worth attending to' is a positive term. So if the term 'work of art' is to be used evaluatively as well as descriptively, which is my claim, then we must account for how a work of art can be bad.

First, we need to look more closely at the ways in which critics talk evaluatively. Critics do, of course, make use of "critical" or derogatory terms such as 'inferior', 'bad', 'second-rate'. But usually their disapprobation is more subtle. Thus we find Ballo's censure, this time of Cesare Macarri's *King Victor Emmanuel Receiving the Plebiscite of the People of Rome* (1870, Siena, Palazzo Pubblico):

> In this 'historical' painting, which was so popular in the last decade of the nineteenth century, the dominant features are the event itself and the craftsman skill displayed by the artist, who, although influenced by David, does not succeed in creating a truly rhythmical synthesis or achieving originality in his style.[2]

The terms 'feature the event itself', 'unrhythmical', and 'unoriginal', (at least prior to the influence of the Romantics) are not in and of themselves necessarily negative, in the way 'bad', 'inferior', or 'second-rate' are. That we understand them as such is due to the context in which these terms appear. We learn elsewhere in the text that simple display of an event, for example, is not enough. And in this passage itself we are given a clue as to why 'unrhythmical' and 'unoriginal' are terms denoting negative traits: rhythm and originality are things which an artist *succeeds* in creating; hence Maccari is considered an unsuccessful artist.

Of course we often find critics telling us that things are bad, probably most often in journalistic criticism—newspaper, magazine, radio, TV reviews— where we are advised or enjoined to spend or not to spend, money and time seeing a film or reading a book.

> It is tempting to describe *March or Die* as this month's Catherine Deneuve movie. The French actress has appeared on-screen so often in the past year or so that one suspects scientists have discovered the secret of duplicating her mesmerizing face on lifelike robots . . . all looking lovely and mysteri-

ous, and all giving remote-control performances that are just this side of catatonic.[3]

But there is, unfortunately for our analysis, very little extended discussion of really bad works in history and criticism. Most critics share the attitude that Northrop Frye expresses in the following passage, that so-called bad works deserve to remain outside the main focus of criticism:

> This coincides with a feeling we have all had: that the study of mediocre works of art remains a random and peripheral form of critical experience, whereas the profound masterpiece draws us to a point at which we seem to see an enormous number of converging patterns of significance.[4]

But this attitude has had some unfortunate consequences. Students would, I think, benefit from studying failures. Once, when I visited Paris with my then twelve-year-old son, I asked him to find the ugliest thing sold at the tourist shops. The "honor" went to the item pictured in plate VI. I believe he learned as much from that exercise as he did from our trips to the Louvre. It is easier to recognize the presence of some property in something when we can also recognize its absence elsewhere. "Converging patterns of significance" become easier to pinpoint when we examine objects in which no such convergence occurs.

What is lacking is much in the way of *study* of the bad. Most readers will probably agree, for example, that Walter Keane's big-eyed children paintings are awful. They, or their imitations, confront us everywhere (outside academe)—in supermarkets and drugstores—and as decorative motifs have become nearly as omnipresent as owls. But try to find a slide for class study in an art-history slide collection, or an article on his work in the art library. I finally found a reference in *Readers' Guide to Periodical Literature* to *Newsweek*, 2 March 1964. According to the *Newsweek* article, it seems that Keane's "Tomorrow Forever" (*not* pictured) was chosen as the theme painting of the Pavilion of Education at the World's Fair in New York, as "something which would be symbolic for the aspiration of children."[5] Critics were generally horrified. We also learn that Keane, an ex–real estate broker who annually grosses, with his wife, more than two million dollars from their works, took out an ad in the August 1963 issue of *Art in America* saying that negotiations were underway for a fair exhibition. Yet the person who has been so successful in winning the aesthetic approval of masses of Americans has been totally ignored in the nonadvertising pages of that journal. Nor do the Keanes' names appear as entries in any of the standard dictionaries or encyclopedias of American art or artists. I was thus not successful in obtaining a copy of

Fig. 14. Lee, *Seated Girl*. University of Minnesota Photo Lab.

"Tomorrow Forever" to include in this book. Instead I had a copy made of a picture by Lee (first name unknown) which I purchased in a drugstore. (See figure 14.) This obvious imitation of the Keanes' work exemplifies their success with the public at large.

The explanation for the neglect of bad art by serious scholars is actually very straightforward. Historians and critics cannot talk about everything; in particular, they do not discuss what they consider not worth discussing.

We do sometimes find critics and historians using inferior works in the way I have suggested, as a background or basis of comparison for superior works. Lorenz Eitner, for example, introduces his study of Géricault's *Raft of the Medusa* by citing it as an outstanding exception to the generally weak exhibition in which it originally appeared, the Salon of 1819.

> The French School had been stagnant for at least a decade. Its younger members practised the routines of classicism without strong conviction. The public, deeply conditioned by habit, accepted the classicist stereotypes as inevitable. . . . Some critics of the Salon sensed this, and recognized in the ease with which the artists had suited their work to the demands of the day, in the facility with which they had turned out insipid altarpieces on commission, the signs of artistic bankruptcy. The French School had, in fact, become too pliable in essentials and too rigid in matters of form; it was held together not by principles, but by platitudes. . . . In an exhibition filled with obsequious expressions of loyalty, it [*The Raft*] affronted the government, spurned official piety, and offered nothing to national pride. It blotted out the pallid fictions which covered the walls around it by the energy with which it concentrated on a horrible fact taken from modern reality.[6]

A further notable exception is Ballo's *The Critical Eye*, a work which has already been cited several times. Although I do not find his concept of 'rhythm' completely clear, Ballo does make an important attempt to explain the term by giving the reader examples of things which lack it as well as examples of things which possess it. In this he accomplishes something many critics don't even seem to consider worth attempting. For example, in discussing Modigliani he says.

> When the movement is created solely by the pose, by a superficial attitude, it is easy to see that it is not real rhythm, which is always based on the concreteness of relationships, of chiaroscuro, colour, lines, and spatial modulations. On occasions its beats and pauses may be subdued and barely perceptible at a first glance, but it always asserts itself as the hidden breath and life of the work.[7]

He shows us *both* a real and a fake Modigliani, and we do begin to understand what he means by 'rhythm', far better than we could have, given only the "rhythmical" work. Readers, especially students self-conscious and unsure of themselves, must find it frustrating not to see the rhythm (or whatever critical aspect) in Michelangelo's work, knowing as they do that it must be there even if they can't see it. One may disagree with some of Ballo's judgments—for example, he finds Thorvaldsen's neoclassicism cold and lifeless, whereas I find his *Christ* neither of these. (See figure 13.) But knowing that such disagreement exists, students are in a better position to investigate for themselves.

Aesthetics does, of course, abound with theories of goodness and beauty (and criticisms of them), but usually only by implication do we find theories of badness and ugliness. Often a theory of what constitutes good art follows immediately from a proposed definition of 'art'. Thus if, for example, art consists in the fulfillment of a particular function, the communication of feelings of brotherhood, for instance, then good works of art can be identified as those which produce those feelings in abundance.

Other theorists, those who deny that art has one and only one function, still insist that the particular function of an individual art work is often relevant to its evaluation. Hence Ballo believes that the Arc de Triomphe (see chapter 2), which might be considered ugly in itself, is "vindicated" by its function of decorating the meeting point of several busy city streets. (See figure 11.) Likewise it is often maintained that what is good for, or in, one art form is not necessarily good in, or for, another:

> [Luigi Rossi's *Orfeo*] illustrates the change that had come over the opera libretto during the first half of the seventeenth century. The antique simplicity of the myth is almost totally buried under a mass of irrelevant incidents and characters, spectacular scenic effects, and incongruous comic episodes. The intrusion of the comic, the grotesque, and the merely sensational into a supposedly serious drama was a common practice of Italian librettists during most of the seventeenth century. It was an indication that the integrity of the drama was no longer of first importance, as it had been with the early Florentines and Monteverdi, and that the ancient Greek and Roman myths had come to be regarded as merely conventional material to be elaborated upon in any way that promised to provide entertainment and offer good opportunities to the composer and singers. The decline of the libretto coincided with the development of an imposing style of theatre music. Rossi's *Orfeo* is, in effect, a succession of beautiful arias and ensembles well calculated to make the hearer forgive its faults as a drama.[8]

There are instances of theories of beauty or goodness which are based upon *appropriateness*, theories which, like so many others, have been discussed since Plato. But even if appropriateness is identified with goodness, matters are not settled. For example, the melody of the first "Gloria" in Puccini's *Missa di Gloria* reminded me, the first time I heard it, of the finale to *Oklahoma!*, and I was bothered by the fact that such a tune was used as the setting for "Gloria in excelsis Deo." But is it fair to say that the joy one feels toward God and the joy felt upon learning that one's territory has become a state are inappropriately expressed in similar music? If so, how does one prove this?

We also find any number of subjective theories of artistic goodness, many of them centering upon the psychology of the viewer. Goodness and pleasure are related fundamentally in such theories: good art is that from which the audience derives pleasure. The variations on this theme are practically endless. Psychoanalytic theories, to cite just one type, add that we derive our pleasure from specific sorts of things. The artist, according to Freud, is elaborating his daydreams so that they lose their idiosyncratic character and can be enjoyed by others. As C. S. Lewis says, this is a theory of reading as well as writing. We read things we enjoy and what we enjoy is daydreams that are shareable. Lewis's criticism of this view points out a weakness often cited by people who reject hedonistic aesthetic theories:

> In order to explain the symbols which they themselves insist on we must admit that humanity is interested in many other things besides sex, and that admission is the thin edge of the wedge. Once it is allowed that our enjoyment of *Paradise Lost* Book IV, is a compound of erotic interest and real though conscious interest in gardens, then it becomes impossible to say *a priori* in what proportion the two are mixed. And even if it could be shown that the latent erotic interest was as 90 and the interest in gardens as 10, that 10 would still be the subject of literary criticism. For clearly the 10 is what distinguishes one poem from another—the 90 being a monotonous continuum spread under all our reading alike and affording no ground for the distinction we usually draw between banality and freshness, dullness and charm, ugliness and beauty. For we must remember that a story about a golden dragon plucking the apple of immortality in a garden at the world's end, and a dream about one's pen going through the paper while one scribbles a note, are, in Freudian terms, the same story. But they are not the same as literature.[9]

Of course, this is in no way intended as a survey, let alone an analysis, of theories of artistic value; there are, of course, many, many theories of other sorts, which I have not mentioned at all. The important point here is not which theories are to be preferred or in what way or ways they all fail. It is, rather, to emphasize the point that evaluation is one aspect of criticism, and that these theories of evaluation imply a distinction between, and hence the existence of, both good and bad works of art. Any definition of 'art' which precludes bad art, then, must be suspect.

Not the least of our worries is the fact that we are faced with disagreement about which things are good and which things are bad. Following an article on the contemporary painter Jasper Johns, these comments appeared in the "letters" section of an issue of *Newsweek:*

> If Jasper Johns (Art, Oct. 24) bronzed your Oct. 24 issue, then painted it, the portrait couldn't be any better than your cover story. George R. Jolliff, Purdy, Mo.
>
> If Jasper Johns can command $270,000 for his brand of art, then I have a garage door I've been wiping paint brushes on for twenty years that is worth a million bucks. Frank Abbott, Washington, D.C.
>
> Thank you for your fine article. As an artist I'm pleased to see art brought into the consciousness of the public so that people may at last lose their misconception about modern art and begin to understand and enjoy it. Catherine Hawks, Mount Pleasant, Mich.
>
> Who is pulling our legs—Mr. Johns or your art editor? G. L. W. Boswell, Nairobi.[10]

These letters show how widespread and heated the debate can be—and how seriously the matter of art is taken (these letters appear just before a group concerning Carter's foreign policy); and these are battles waged not simply within academe or the institutional art world.

The matter of public taste has puzzled a great many theorists. Hume asserted that everyone who had read both Milton and Ogilby would agree that Milton is the better poet.[11] And I find it hard to believe that anyone who has seen Marina Kondratieva dance Michel Fokine's choreography of Saint-Saëns's "Death of a Swan" will claim that the performance was ugly. But will everyone who has seen the paintings both of Keane and Johns agree that Johns is the better painter? Obviously not, if we are to take these letters and supermarket sales seriously.

The concept of taste has played a very important role in aesthetics since the eighteenth-century British empiricists made it the center of their theories.[12] It is in many ways a very appealing notion, for it at once serves both the objective and subjective sides of aesthetic judgment. This dual role is best understood, I think, if we follow the eighteenth-century empiricists' suggestion that taste is analogous with sight. Human beings all have the sense of sight, goes this argument, but do not always agree about what they see; for some people have defective visual mechanisms and some are more highly trained than others. Further, temperaments and mood often affect what we see. Even a person with perfect vision may, due to lack of experience or mental disturbance, be unable to see something which is visible to those with less nearly perfect vision. The objectivity of sight ("That apple really is red") is based in our common possession of the sense; the subjectivity of our judgments based upon it is due to individual differences. Similarly, aesthetic taste was considered a natural faculty, with differences in sensitivity and experience accounting for disagreements. Thus Hume said, "The general principles of taste are uniform in human nature: Where men vary in their judgments, some defect or perversion in the faculties may commonly be remarked; proceeding either from prejudice, from want of practice, or want of delicacy; and there is just reason for approving one taste, and condemning another."[13]

Disagreements like the one about the value of Jasper Johns's work are, like ethical disagreements, particularly unsettling. When we discover people disagreeing about the age of one of their friends, we do not find them concluding that the person's age is therefore "just a matter of personal opinion." And we like, too, to believe there is some sort of objective truth about a work of art's merit; we like to believe that at some point we can conclude "this work of art is bad," just as we may say "that apple is red." But we are often unsure ourselves what this objective truth about a work of art might be. The fact that a carnival worker's beliefs about my height and weight differ from my own certainly does not lead me to doubt my own judgment. Yet all of us will probably confess to occasional doubts concerning the reliability of our own aesthetic judgments; we look, as Hume suggested, to those whose aesthetic senses are said to be more highly developed. We have even invented and conventionalized ways of protecting ourselves: some books, for example, books we have read with thorough enjoyment, we only describe to friends as "a good thing to read on an airplane" or "some of my trash reading." In a well-known essay, "High-Brows and Low Brows," C. S. Lewis describes a prep school which made in its library a distinction between "books" and "good books." Lewis goes on to ask why so many of the serious, classical, literary volumes found in the "good books" section are so often thought to be bad by the majority of readers. He discusses Rider Haggard's *She* as a candidate for a good, bad book—a book of some merit which we would nevertheless call "bad" or "lowbrow." The story is a good quest story, the characters are consistent, and the plot is plausible. But it has two weaknesses: She, the title character, says things that are shallow and foolish; and there is a "continuous poverty of style"—"a sloth or incompetence of writing whereby the author is content always with a vague approximation to the emotion, the reflection, or the image he intends, so that a certain smudging and banality is spread over all."[14] He concludes that from this it follows that *She* is not a bad, good book or a good, bad book but a book that is bad and good. But his discussion also demonstrates that most of us are very sensitive to other people's judgments. We sheepishly enjoy what we know are "bad" books; we must often force ourselves to read the classics—those works that others have judged "good" for us.

We are sensitive to the aesthetic judgments of others, and yet we are often reluctant to impose our own judgments on someone else. We all know people who put the most incredible things on the walls of their homes or in their gardens. If my father saw a neighbor making a mistake in installing a new window, he would not hesitate to tell him the correct way to do it. My brother would interfere if he saw that neighbor kicking a dog. Neither made a single remark (nor did I) when that same neighbor installed the bird-bath pictured in plate VII. We often rationalize such behavior by saying that, unlike the incorrectly installed window or kicked dog, ugly bird baths "do no real harm." The superiority we feel provides its own satisfaction; we do not feel that action is required. Gombrich cites the example of a pope who ordered that art works be sprinkled with gold in order to make them better. Our reaction to this is quite different from our reaction to the popes who ordered executions or the suppression of scientific writings. As Gombrich explains:

> The taste that is here ridiculed is the "vulgar" taste of the Philistine, and it only adds spice to Vasari's story that this Philistine is the Pope himself, who thus proves himself inferior in culture to the artists he employs. There is no need to add further examples. For in the strict hierarchic society of the sixteenth and seventeenth centuries the contrast between the "vulgar" and the "noble" becomes one of the principle preoccupations of the critics. Not that they recognized this contrast for a metaphor. On the contrary. Their belief was that certain forms or modes are "really" vulgar, because they please the low, while others are inherently noble, because only a developed taste can appreciate them. Their examples of what constitutes "decorum" always point in the same direction. There is always a strong negative element in what constitutes "good taste." It presupposes a mind not easily swayed by the appeal of immediate gratification which would be a lure to the "vulgar." Thus loud colours, provacative dress, expletive speech, are all a "breach of decorum" and in bad taste.[15]

Yet there are those (and Gombrich is himself undoubtedly among them) who consider bad taste more serious than a mere breach of decorum. For the critics, bad taste is a corrupting influence, something that does, perhaps, deserve correction. Ballo, for instance, discusses what he considers the insidious effect of bad works of art:

> The formation of this early kind of taste is influenced by the things we see around us, which become our teachers without our knowing it. They may range from the products of craftsmen to mass-produced articles; from trivial knickknacks to picture-postcards, commonplace images of saints, Christmas cards and strip cartoons; from the appalling statues to be seen in cemeteries to advertisements and the ugly monuments in our public squares. All these things, to which no critic attaches any importance, have a fundamental influence on the formation of taste, a greater influence than real works of art, which are comparatively rare and which few people ever see or study—or if they do see them, do so without knowing how to look at them.[16]

(I like to think that Ballo would say something to a neighbor who put a pink plaster-of-Paris flamingo in his garden.)

Might we then try to use taste as a means of making the concept of bad art consistent with my proposed definition of 'art'? Some people think some properties are worth attending to, some concentrate instead on other properties. The properties critics cherish also vary from time to time, from culture to culture. We could, perhaps, simply consider the kinds of "properties worth attending to" a matter of choice or taste; we would postulate that viewers with "good taste" will recognize good works of art. Such a definition would state: x is a good (bad) work of art if and only if

> (1) x is an artifact and (2) information concerning the history of production of x will direct the viewer's attention to properties which the viewer considers worth attending to and (3) the viewer has good (bad) taste.

Unfortunately, this way out depends upon our being able to explain what "good taste" is, and I doubt that this is possible. How do we tell who has really developed it? How can it be cultivated? Aesthetic or artistic taste is, after all, not really another sense. Sight can be tested and, to some extent, corrected. But both testing and correction are problematic where taste is concerned. Suppose the examinee were given one of Dickens's works to read. As Forster indicates, it is hard to draw any conclusions about the person who says, "This is bad."

> Part of the genius of Dickens is that he does use types and caricatures, people whom we recognize the instant they re-enter, and yet achieves effects that are not mechanical and a vision of humanity that is not shallow.

> Those who dislike Dickens have excellent taste. He ought to be bad. He is
> actually one of our big writers, and his immense success with types suggests
> that there may be more in flatness than the severer critics admit.[17]

"This is bad," seems here to be consistent with both excellent and poor taste,
and if the conclusion is, "This is good," how can we be sure that the person is
really exercising taste at all? Might he or she not simply know independently
that Dickens is highly thought of?

If we test taste by using works already identified as "the greats," we run the
risk of choosing something that the subject *knows* is supposed to be good.
Hence we will not be able to determine whether he or she is actually exercising *taste* at all, let alone good taste. In the Dickens case we run into the
additional problem that highly complex works may have high and low points
(or at least higher and lower points) and a simple answer to the question "Do
you like it?" may be particularly hard to give exactly for those persons with the
"best taste." Choosing simpler examples won't help. Finding out how people
react to single words or colors, or to simple arrangements of them, will not
help us anticipate their reactions to more complex works.

Furthermore, we must ask how we could decide that an example should be
used in our test. Either we already know that people of good or bad taste like
it—presupposing a standard of taste—or we have other grounds for saying that
it is good or bad, in which case the concept of taste is unnecessary.

For these reasons I prefer to account for bad art by means of something
other than taste. I. A. Richards proposes one solution. In a short chapter,
"Badness in Poetry," in his *Principles of Literary Criticism*, Richards develops
his poetics around another mental phenomenon, "attitude." Poetry, he says—
unlike science, which organizes beliefs—organizes attitudes. The value of a
poem is determined by the extent to which it organizes attitudes *and* by the
particular attitudes involved: "Sometimes art is bad because communication is
defective, the vehicle is inoperative: sometimes because the experience com-
municated is worthless: sometimes for both reasons."[18] Consider Richards's
analysis of the following "bad poem":

The Pool

Are you alive?
I touch you.
You quiver like a sea-fish,
I cover you with my net.
What are you—banded one?

"The Pool" is bad, or ineffective, says Richards, because it is unduly brief, simple, tenuous, and ambiguous. A reader will experience something upon reading the poem, but will not experience anything as specific as successful poems draw out. As Richards explains, "Had the poet said only, 'I went and poked about for rocklings and caught the pool itself,' the reader, who converts [this] into a poem, would still have been able to construct an experience of equal value, for what results is almost independent of the author."[19]

What Richards calls "stock responses" are responsible for the fact that anything concrete results from this bad poem, that the reader experiences anything at all. "As general reflection develops, the place of the free direct play of experience is taken by the deliberate organization of attitudes, a clumsy and crude substitute."[20] Readers hold certain conventional ideas (for example, love, friendship, summer, youth) and it is these ideas which constitute the greater part of our responses to life in general, art in particular. Mediocre poetry, which Richards thinks is exemplified by one of Ella Wheeler Wilcox's sonnets, depends for what success it has upon the existence of these stock responses:

> After the fierce midsummer all ablaze
>   Has burned itself to ashes and expires
>   In the intensity of its own fires,
> Then come the mellow, mild, St. Martin days
> Crowned with the calm of peace, but sad with haze.
>   So after Love has led us, till he tires
>   Of his own throes and torments, and desires,
> Comes large-eyed Friendship: with a restful gaze
> He beckons us to follow, and across
>   Cool, verdant vales we wander free from care.
>   Is it a touch of frost lies in the air?
> Why are we haunted with a sense of loss?
>   We do not wish the pain back, or the heat;
>   And yet, and yet, these days are incomplete.

Great poetry goes beyond them, making the reader respond in new ways, ways which demonstrate the ineffectiveness and inadequacy of stock responses for dealing with the richness of experience. However, most readers never get beyond the stage of reacting in stock or standard ways. Like Ballo, Richards sees this as a result of the aesthetically deprived environment in which most people find themselves:

At present bad literature, bad art, the cinema, etc., are an influence of the first importance in fixing immature and actually inapplicable attitudes to most things. Even the decision as to what constitutes a pretty girl or a handsome young man, an affair apparently natural and personal enough, is largely determined by magazine covers and movie stars. The quite common opinion that the arts have after all very little effect upon the community shows only that too little attention is being paid to the effects of bad art.[21]

The superiority of poetry which derives its effectiveness from something beyond stock responses is "proved" (though Richards admits not strictly) by the fact that people who read and comprehend it are no longer satisfied with standard fare: "The fact that those who have passed through the stage of enjoying the *Poems of Passion* to that of enjoying the bulk of the contents of the *Golden Treasury*, for example, do not return, settles the matter."[22]

I believe, however, that 'attitude' is not much better than 'taste' for our needs. It is not a clear concept. Further, Richards's test of goodness (What do people who have read both the *Golden Treasury* and *Poems of Passion* prefer?) is very similar to that which Hume suggests in "Of the Standard of Taste," and relies again upon the troublesome concept of a competent judge (Richards's "good critic"). A poem is good if and only if good critics—people of educated taste and broad experience—say so. But like Hume, Richards admits that even good critics (competent judges) can go wrong at times: "Even a good critic at a sufficiently low ebb of natural potency might mistake such a sonnet [Wilcox's] for one of Shakespeare's or with more ease for one of Rossetti's."[23] The mere fact that a person has tasted both beer and brandy and prefers the latter does not prove that brandy is the better drink. What we are reduced to is saying that a poem is good if and only if a competent judge judging competently says so. But how are we to know when a competent judge is judging competently? It must be because he or she picks out the best poem. But this, of course, is a circular argument, or it shows us that we have a standard of goodness independent of the judge.

In practice we circumvent this difficulty by appealing not to a single judge, but to a group of them. We ask for the opinion of the majority of critics, in the hope that most of them are not at a low ebb. And as we have seen, we listen attentively to what they say in hopes of gaining richer aesthetic experiences. But we still retain the right to decide for ourselves whether an art work is good or bad. And even if we admit that what is considered art varies as taste varies, we still want to be able to say that some art is bad *now*.

An adequate theory of aesthetic value must finally come, I believe, not from empirical theories of viewer behavior (either general viewers or competent viewers), but somehow from the works themselves, from their own inherent properties. But how can we develop such a theory? Compare, for example, the Rockwell paintings (especially *The Marriage License*) and the Vermeer (figures 15 and 16). Which work is more appealing? Which is of greater artistic merit? These will not be simple questions to answer. The relative

Fig. 15. Jan Vermeer, *Maidservant Pouring Milk*. Rijksmuseum Amsterdam.

Fig. 16. Norman Rockwell, *The Marriage License*. Courtesy, The Old Corner House, Stockbridge Historical Society, Stockbridge, Massachusetts.

reputation of each artist (and each artist's work) is well known. Vermeer is, of course, almost universally admired. But Rockwell, though he is an immensely popular illustrator—one who would be identified as a fine artist by a majority of Americans—is a man whom most sophisticated critics and historians despise or simply neglect.[24] References to Rockwell are almost as rare in academia as are references to Keane. (I did find one Rockwell slide in the University of Minnesota Art History Department slide library, and six in the Home Economics School's Department of Design.) But putting aside for the moment the reputation each work has inherited, can we independently—that is, independently of general critical opinion—determine for ourselves which is the superior work?

We might first begin by suggesting that one art work fits into a tradition of great art, while the other does not. Perhaps this is what distinguishes the great artists from lesser ones; great artists borrow from others, their works reverberate with echoes from other masters. Perhaps lesser works may be distinguished by a poverty of such reference. But assuming that the Rockwell painting really is an instance of mediocre art, we find we cannot call it so on this basis. Rockwell himself notes that he is indeed indebted to the great artists of the past:

> I can't say who has influenced me really. Or at least I can't say how the artists I have admired have influenced me. Some of those I admire—Picasso, for example—have had no discernible effect (to say the least) on my work. Ever since I can remember, Rembrandt has been my favorite artist. Vermeer, Breughel, Velasquez, Cavaletto, Dürer, Holbein, Ingres as draftsman; Matisse, Klee, these are a few of the others I admire now. During my student days I studied closely the works of Edwin Austin Abbey, J. C. and Frank Leyendecker, Howard Pyle, Sargent and Whistler.[25]

That Rockwell has borrowed directly from some masters is indisputable. (Compare, for example, *Rosie the Riveter* with Michelangelo's *Isaiah* in the Sistine Chapel, figures 17 and 18.) And he shares many of his interests—in his use of light, and in the middle class, for instance—with artists like Vermeer. Why then is Vermeer the better painter?[26]

Perhaps we can find the answer by comparing the technique of each painting. If we cannot fault *what* he depicts, then it must be in the *how* of his depiction that his weakness lies. It is not merely the content (big-eyed children) that accounts for badness—if it were we would have to put Reynolds's *Strawberry Girl* in the heap with the works of the Keanes and their followers (compare figures 19 and 14). Rudolf Arnheim asks:

Fig. 17. Michelangelo, *The Prophet Isaiah*. Musei Vaticani.

Fig. 18. Norman Rockwell, *Rosie the Riveter*. Reprinted from The Saturday Evening Post, © 1943, The Curtis Publishing Company.

Fig. 19. Sir Joshua Reynolds, *Strawberry Girl*. Reproduced by permission of the Trustees of the Wallace Collection, London.

When we pick up an object on the beach because of its regular shape, why do we throw it away, disappointed and contemptuous, when it turns out to be a factory-made comb or can? We do so because the simplicity of the factory product is cheaply achieved. It is not wrested from the forces of nature but forced upon matter from the outside.[27]

And Ballo comments:

The ordinary man finds that there is little difference between a picture postcard and Utrillo's painting [*House of the Composer Berlioz*], and in fact, up to a few years ago, he would have been inclined to give the preference to the postcard on account of its shallow sentimentality and he would have described the Utrillo as "childish." In reality, Utrillo's painting shows that he was a real artist, since he knows how to use tones and with the aid of colours evokes a lyrical state of mind.[28]

Both of these comments suggest that artistic superiority depends upon craftsmanship. Certainly insufficient craftsmanship is what makes us disregard the poetry of the Scot McGonagall:

Ye lovers of the picturesque, if ye would drown your grief,
Take my advice and visit the ancient town of Crieff;
The climate is bracing, and the walks lovely to see,
Besides, ye can ramble over the district and view the beautiful scenery

As James Holroyd comments, his poetry is pleasant, but ordinary and unskilled:

He praised the resorts for their pure air, for their public parks, and for their plentiful supply of water where visitors could quench their thirst gratis. McGonagall plays endless variations on these poor man's pleasures in a vocabulary that was sincere though repetitious. The prospects were always most lovely or most beautiful to be seen, the grass always green, the visitors' hearts light and gay as they drove dull care away throughout the livelong summer day.[29]

We appreciate products of human skill, knowing that they were difficult to come by. Great artists possess knowledge and techniques which most of us lack and admire; we are unlikely to like a pedestrian poem which we ourselves could have written. Artists of stature know, for example, how to use tones, how to use light, or color, or language in some special way.

Vermeer, for instance, is often extolled for the way in which he represents light, particularly the way in which it is reflected by objects of different materials and textures. Dots or points of light are picked up and reflected (look carefully at figure 15, *Interior with a Maidservant Pouring Milk*) by buttons, the pitcher on the table, baskets on the wall, the tablecloth, the milk, and the bread. People familiar with the work of Vermeer are accustomed to looking in his pictures for these sources of light, and find great satisfaction in the way he handles them.

Yet we find that Rockwell renders light in similar ways. In *Marriage License*, he uses, in fact, many of Vermeer's techniques. The daylight from the window has the central position in his painting, whereas Vermeer does not usually include the source of light (and Vermeer generally places a window to one side of a scene). But neither lets the light from the window take over; like Vermeer, Rockwell lets the light reflect variously upon the many objects in the scene. One of my students described the work as follows:

> First outlining the window pans and frame, and stopping to dot nails and shutters, the light is then caught by the young couple worrying over the legal papers. It brightens their faces and sharpens their features. It travels across the man's shoulder and down the woman's dress to her lifted heels. The yellow dress seems almost electric in its brilliance, contrasted to the deep brown of most of the room's furnishings. It is picked up again in dots of a light or fan pullchain (concealed) suspended from the ceiling, reminiscent of the string of pearls in Vermeer's painting. Again on the old stove, the spots of light outline the heavy iron, separating it from the darkness. The highlights spread down the length of it and are picked up again in the low center of the picture by a spittoon and discarded cigarette filters. Next it travels to catch two white paws of an almost hidden kitchen, its neck and the tip of its nose. It spots the clerk's shoes and highlights his exposed stocking. The dots appear again on the wooden rungs of his chair. A major source of reflected light in the scene is the clerk's hung coat and hat, and rests on the window frame again.
>
> The effect is subtle but substantial. As it travels around this otherwise dead interior, light decorates the form it touches. It gives substance, creating a real physical world, as it does in Vermeer's world. Almost as though another presence in the room, the light takes inventory of the space, even while the figures take no notice.[30]

Perhaps we can now look more favorably at Rockwell's work. Yet still, when we compare it with the Vermeer, is it found lacking? If so, why? Perhaps the subject matter of each painting will provide the answer. Can we say that the subject of the Rockwell painting is trivial, the subject of the Vermeer profound?

Rockwell's admirers are particularly on the defensive in this matter. Thus in her preface to a book on Rockwell, Dorothy Canfield Fisher provides an apology of a sort we would never find in a contemporary book on Vermeer:

> I have recently written a defence of those serious and sincere modern
> authors who attempt to understand and portray what they see in American
> life, even if their report is shocking to those who never come in contact with
> filth and moral degradation. My argument is that if, in American life, such
> sordidness and misery are often found, nothing is gained by pretending in
> books that things in our country are different from what they are. Having
> gone on record publicly with this claim of the right of an honest portrayer of
> human life to give us his report, even if it sickens us, I think I have the right
> to make the same claim for another honest portrayer of human lie even if his
> report cheers and comforts us.[31]

Fisher goes on to suggest that Rockwell is a victim of the "see-saw of aesthetic
fashion."[32] It is not that his work is bad, but rather than it does not relate well
to social concerns of the kind currently foremost in our national consciousness.

> It is true that, in our country, minorities suffer from savagely unjust dis-
> criminations, that there are shocking inequalities of opportunity which
> cause widespread human misery. But in our America there are also—so
> familiar that a portrayal of them gives to millions the pleasure of recogni-
> tion—uncountable homes, warm with love and trust, and with thankfulness
> of the shelter, in the very midst of the typhoon of human struggle, which
> such homes give to those who live in them.[33]

Fisher wants it both ways at once. She claims that the national consciousness
is focused on the ugly side of American life, yet this is not consistent with
Rockwell's great popularity. It must be only certain consciousnesses in the
nation, namely those of academics, critics, and journalists, those who dismiss
Rockwell, who are concentrating on the shocking inequalities. Obviously
there will be no "pleasure of recognition" for those who believe that the
warmth and trust depicted by Rockwell is a sham. In explaining the appeal
Rockwell has for him, Arthur L. Guptill says, "Because Rockwell breathed
affection into his paintings, they aroused affect in the heart of the beholder,
and one was dull indeed who did not comprehend that the Common Man was
quite an uncommon fellow."[34] A possible explanation is that the critic is not a
common man, but a dullard or person of stone whose affection cannot be
roused. This is, however, a vary serious indictment of those who do not like
Rockwell—and, I think, false. Not everyone who finds something lacking in
Rockwell believes that he literally "paints a false picture" of American life, or
is totally unable to react emotionally to his works.

The charge of "lack of relevance"—or of breadth of appeal, universality of
subject matter—is one that is often leveled at so-called lesser works of art.
Irving Sandler, for instance, explains his disapproval of Regionalism:

In a decade of widespread farm foreclosures and monopolization, the Regionalist conception of America as a paradise of independent small farmers and townsmen came to seem as incredible fantasy. As America's outlook turned global, Regionalism . . . lost its pertinence.[35]

The political pertinence Sandler has in mind is only one kind—and a narrow one at that—of social relevance. The sort that F. R. Leavis insists is necessary for great works, a "depth of interest in humanity" and an "intensity of moral preoccupation,"[36] is much more encompassing. Could the problem be that Rockwell lacks this? Rockwell's own remarks on this subject are revealing. Describing the genesis of one of his works, he says,

> I think I have always wanted to paint a charwoman or some similar type of worker—the poor little drudge who has to tidy up after more fortunate people have had a good time. I've been interested in the hotel maid, for instance, who has to lay out her ladyship's gown; in reality the maid may be more of a lady—but let's not get into the social angle.[37]

Rockwell's last "but let's not get into the social angle," is indeed strange. But it must mean that he does not want to *discuss* in words the social angle, not that he does not want to include it in his painting, for this "angle" must occur to people who look at the painting. We simply cannot maintain that Rockwell is immoral or amoral, antisocial or asocial, or even that his moral and social beliefs are out of date.

We are still, then, left with our problem. People who admit that Rockwell's paintings are neither devoid of content nor lacking in skill often claim that they "do nothing" for them—that they "leave me cold." The affective theory of art (which we have already considered to some extent in connection with Richards and Tolstoy) demands that art affect its viewers. The really great artists, goes this line of reasoning, are those who affect us greatly. Helen Vendler, for one, believes that great art affects our lives profoundly.

> It was uttered by Rilke through his oracular archaic torso of Apollo, and it is the demand that we change our life. Not all poets put that demand in the same way as Rilke, but in each poet there is a testimony speaking of the irresistible and undeniable rearrangement of the mind brought about by the confrontation with achieved aesthetic beauty.[38]

We do occasionally hear that a particular work of art has changed someone's life. But this way of distinguishing good art from bad art is plagued with unanswered questions. How great must the change be? Must a work change the life of everyone who perceives it in order to be good? A majority? Probably a majority of Americans would say that they are moved by Rockwell's work.

Must we resort again to the competent judge? If someone says his or her life was changed after looking at Rockwell's *Marriage License* but not by Vermeer's *Interior with a Maidservant Pouring Milk*, does it necessarily follow that the former is a better painting? Certainly we can agree that art does affect us. But merely claiming that a work leaves one cold (or the reverse) is not illuminating until we can explain why or how, and how or why this is relevant to an evaluation of a work of art.

Related to the notion of "changing one's life" is the notion—a more manageable one—of influence. Leavis claims that the difference between good and great literature is that the great works act as an influence upon later writers. Thus the "great tradition" is understood in terms of a line of influence from George Eliot through Henry James to Joseph Conrad.[39] I find much that is attractive about this view. It narrows the class of those whose lives must be affected or changed to the class of artists. Further, the change in question has some concrete manifestation: we can see the influence in the works of later artists.

There is, however, a rather serious problem for a theory of goodness which states that a work is good if and only if it exerts influence on other artists. Suppose a painting of the fourteenth century was hidden away immediately after completion, and not discovered until today. If we strictly adhere to Leavis's view, we must conclude that such a painting is not a good one, or at least that it is not a great painting (though we might postulate that it could *become* so). Nor does it help to alter the theory so as to highlight the artist instead: a work is good if and only if it was produced by a person who exerted influence on other artists. Great artists sometimes produce bad works; and a work we discover today may be unidentified with respect to its creator, or may be an artist's only work.

But worse for the problem we have posed, it is not clear how influence comes to the aid of my proposed definition of 'work of art'. We might add a third condition:

> x is a good (bad) work of art if and only if (1) x is an artifact and (2) information concerning the history of production of x will direct the viewer's attention to properties worth attending to and (3) x exerts (does not exert) influence on artists.

I do not think (putting aside the problems discussed in the last paragraph) that this is necessarily incorrect. But it is difficult to see why only some works with properties worth attending to exert influence while others do not. Even if it is the case that one of the reasons that Rockwell is not taken seriously by critics is that his influence has not been great enough, is this not a symptom rather than a cause? The question still to be answered is this: Are there properties worth attending to in Rockwell's paintings or aren't there? If there are, aren't the paintings works of art and automatically good? Surely moral content, craftsmanship, and affectiveness are properties worth pointing to. Can it be that they are not enough?

There is a clue, I think, to the solution of this puzzle in Arnheim's phrase, "cheaply achieved." Gombrich mentions the same word in a related context: "The main objection against the Victorian interior is that it is 'vulgar,' by which is meant that it allows a too easy childish gratification in the gaudy and 'cheap.' "[40] It is not surprising that the Boy Scouts of America chose Norman Rockwell to illustrate their annual calendars. Guptill remarks, "He recognized the significance of the Scouts' character building program, believing that helpfulness and consideration for others are things the world can use a lot of."[41] Of course we all agree that helpfulness and consideration for others are things the world can use. But Rockwell's visual statement of this is cheaply achieved. It is childish—fine for Boy Scout calendars, but not art for adults. As Leavis says, fortunately there are some books that have been written for adults, works which have "unusual and sustained seriousness."[42] Leavis has in mind, I think, something very close to what I mean when I say that a work has properties worth attending to. Good works of art require attention just because they are sustainedly serious; they make demands on us that mediocre and childish art do not make.

We might be tempted to say that Rockwell's paintings—or at least some of them—are cartoons (in the contemporary journalistic sense, not as plans for tapestries or other larger works). But even as cartoons they are terribly simple. Most political cartoons, for example, are extremely symbolic in nature, requiring a fair amount of knowledge on the part of the viewer. Compare Rockwell's *Rosie the Riveter* (figure 18) to Daumier's *The Balance of Europe* (figure 8).[43] Daumier's cartoon is obvious—but only to people who are familiar with the political metaphors of their day, just as most Americans in 1980 understand at once the depiction of a confrontation between an elephant on a donkey. But they "get" this only because they are familiar with current symbols and metaphors. Rockwell, on the other hand, is more literal than figurative. He is not a metaphorical, let alone metaphysical, illustrator.

This is not to say that Rockwell's paintings are not at all symbolic. The turkey in *Freedom From Want*, for example, symbolizes *plenty*. But his symbolism is direct and obvious, not at all subtle. Cartoons, says Gombrich, are a "neat summing up."[44] But, I think, they cannot be *too* neat or the cleverness is lost. It is like saying something that everybody already knows in the same way that it has been said before. Guindon's cartoon (see figure 20) says

Fig. 20. Cartoon by Richard Guindon. Minneapolis Tribune.

something that has been said before, but redeems itself by saying it cleverly
and originally. Rockwell's restatements, however, are uninteresting—as uninteresting as the claim, "Helpfulness and consideration for others are things
the world can use a lot of." Terri Alwell is correct in pointing out that
Rockwell's use of light is often "subtle." But the subtlety of the treatment is
overwhelmed by the grossness of the visual statement. Vermeer's "message"
in his painting of the maidservant (see figure 15) is certainly not complex;
often the best poems have the simplest point. But there is a great difference
between being simple and being overstated. In Rockwell's case the overstate-
ment is neither redeemed nor enhanced by his craftsmanship as they are in the
Vermeer. Rockwell might very well have profited from Lewis Carroll's witty
advice:

> Then, if you'd be impressive,
>   Remember what I say,
> That abstract qualities begin
>   With capitals alway:
> The True, the Good, the Beautiful—
>   Those are the things that pay!
>
> Next, when you are describing
>   A shape, or sound, or tint;
> Don't state the matter plainly,
>   But put it in a hint;
> And learn to look at all things
>   With a sort of mental squint.
>
> For instance, if I wished, Sir,
>   Of mutton-pies to tell,
> Should I say "dreams of fleecy flocks
>   Pent in a wheaten cell?"
> "Why, yes," the old man said; "that phrase
>   Would answer very well."[45]

As Arnheim suggests, "The reason why we may hesitate to describe the
average child's drawing or an Egyptian pyramid or certain 'functional' buildings as 'works of art' is precisely that a maximum of complexity, or richness,
seems to be indispensable."[46]

Popular novelists and other popular artists, then, suffer from being too easy
to "read." Sloan Wilson (known primarily for *The Man in the Gray Flannel
Suit*) is a good example. In his novel *All the Best People*, we begin "at the
beginning" and go chronologically through the events of the novel to the end.
Such simplicity of treatment is particularly striking when we compare such a
novel with a more complex one like *The Good Soldier* by Ford Madox Ford.
When we read Wilson's novel, we know that everything in chapter 3 came

before the action of chapter 10. But with Ford's work the reader must pay careful attention in order to know how to piece together the events of the novel.

This is the most complicated time-statement we get in *All the Best People:*

> About every two years for about a decade after that, Caroline started a new business. For the rest of his life he dated events which had taken place during this period to the occupational status of his wife.[47]

It is difficult to pick a passage from *The Good Soldier* which adequately exemplifies its complicated time structure; but the following should serve to suggest the contrast between it and Wilson's work:

> The death of Mrs. Maidan occurred on the 4th of August, 1904. And then nothing happened until the 4th of August, 1913. There is the curious coincidence of dates, but I do not know whether that is one of those sinister, as if half-jocular and altogether merciless proceedings on the part of a cruel Providence that we call a coincidence. Because it may just as well have been the superstitious mind of Florence that forced her to certain acts, as if she had been hypnotized. It is, however, certain that the 4th of August always proved a significant date for her. To begin with, she was born on the 4th of August. Then, on that date, in the year 1899, she set out with her uncle for the tour round the world in company with a young man called Jimmy. But that was not merely a coincidence. Her kindly old uncle, with the supposedly damaged heart, was, in his delicate way, offering her, in this trip, a birthday present to celebrate her coming of age. Then, on the 4th of August, 1900, she yielded to an action that certainly coloured her whole life—as well as mine. She had no luck. She was probably offering herself a birthday present that morning. . . .[48]

In his introduction to Ford's novel, Graham Greene says, "The time-shifts are valuable not merely for purposes of suspense—they lend veracity to the appalling events. This is just how memory does work, and we become involved with the narrator's memory as though it were our own."[49] A great deal, it turns out, happened between 1904 and 1913. But we do not learn about it until much later, just as we do not learn until much later (although it is often referred to) what happened on 4 August 1900. Fitting the pieces together requires the reader's careful attention. The narrator knows full well that a great deal happened. But at this point in the novel he "talks around" these significant events. Thus his remarks are also psychologically revealing; such "gaps" in the chronology serve also to highlight his own inability to deal with some of the unpleasant realities of his life.

It is impossible to draw someone's attention to equally interesting properties in *All the Best People*. It is not just that Wilson doesn't require that his readers piece together the novel's chronology. The characterization is equally obvious. Characters simply do things without adequate motivation or preparation. A rather shy, quiet boy and young man, Dana Campbell, suddenly becomes a first-rate naval commander, exhibiting traits of administrative and executive prowess that we are utterly unprepared for. We are given flat characters, stereotypes. Effects are "achieved cheaply." People supposedly conversing in the 1940s inconsistently use slang from the forties and jargon (like "effete Easterner"), popular not then but in the years when the novel was written. Wilson, like Rockwell, gives us obvious types who are so simple that they are not real or plausible. We are straightforwardly *told* that the people act or look that way; nothing is *shown* to us. In a sense we are told too much. The novel "reads" so easily we are allowed to become lazy. There is no need for us to fill in anything. And we become bored. The old cliché that anything worthwhile requires hard work applies here. Like popular singing groups (The Carpenters, say), Wilson and Rockwell are relaxing, distracting, time-consuming. We hum the tunes mindlessly. We get everything the first time round.

As Gombrich suggests, works of art are satisfying only when they provide some challenge. "We prefer suggestion to representation," he says; "we have adjusted our expectations to enjoy the very act of guessing, of projecting."[50] And in discussing A. W. Bouguereau's *The Birth of Venus* he comments:

> Let us admit right away that Bouguereau has made further progress in the direction of representational accuracy—beyond Raphael, whom he exploits, and beyond Titian. Aided by the successive conquests of appearance made during two centuries and by the mechanical devices of photography, he places before us a most convincing image of a nude model. Why, then, does it make us rather sick? I think the reason is obvious. This is a pin-up girl rather than a work of art. By this we mean that the erotic appeal is on the surface—is not compensated for by the sharing in the artist's imaginative process. The image is painfully easy to read, and we resent being taken for such simpletons. . . .[51]

Evidence of skill and interesting content may be necessary conditions of a work's goodness. A poem like this, lacking both, will immediately be dismissed as "bad":

Morning

I like the morning sunlight
The flowers and the birds
Because it makes me feel like
I'll start this day off right.[52]

"Morning" does not give us the same problems that a Rockwell work does. Its badness is easily explained in terms of lack of craftsmanship. Rockwell's technique is well above average; here the poet demonstrates a minimal ability to manipulate words. And the idea expressed is silly—something not true of Rockwell's work.

But craftsmanship and content are not sufficient to ensure a work's goodness. The viewer must become involved with the work, and this happens only if there is something for him or her to do. It is not just that good works of art possess properties worth attending to; the *attending* itself must be worthwhile. Great works of art are so rich and complex that they lend themselves to unending discussion and analysis. (This is true of Reynolds's *Strawberry Girl*, but not of Lee's little girl. See figures 19 and 14) They cannot be gotten all at once, at first reading, hearing, or glance. As Gombrich says, "the stimulus . . . is of infinite ambiguity."[53] Good works require interpretation and reinterpretation. This is why we sometimes find the critical discussion surrounding a work nearly as interesting as the work itself—and crucial to an artifact's standing as a work of art.

This is the case, I think, with Henry James's *The Turn of the Screw*. This short novel has generated a fascinating debate over whether the central character, a governess, is an innocent victim of evil or a deranged doer of evil herself.[54] It is not that there is simply a puzzle to be solved by the cleverest readers. Equally intelligent and insightful readers differ in their interpretations. The novel lends itself to various critical methods: intentionalistic, psychoanalytic, and formalist. Details await discovery and emphasis for each new reader. A fresh reading can produce interpretations unthought of before. Professor Harold C. Goddard's experience is a striking example:

> What was my surprise, then, on taking it up with a group of students, to discover that not one of them interpreted it as I did. My faith in what seemed to me the obvious way of taking the story would have been shaken, had I not, on explaining it, found the majority of my fellow readers ready to prefer it to their own. And this experience was repeated with later groups. Yet, even after several years, it had not occurred to me that what seemed the natural interpretation of the narrative was not the generally accepted one among critics, however little it might be among students. And then one day I ran on a comment of Mr. Chesterton's on the story. He took it precisely as my students had. I began watching out in my reading for allusions to the story. I looked up several references to it. They all agreed. Evidently my view was utterly heretical. Naturally I asked myself more sharply than ever why I should take the tale as a matter of course in a way that did not seem to occur to other readers. Was it perversity on my part, or profundity?[55]

Probably some of both, though certainly more of the latter. But primarily it is the novel itself that accounts for the debate. And as the debate is waged, readers benefit from having things about the novel pointed out for them that they might otherwise have overlooked.

Bad art does not lend itself to such interesting discussion. Readers do not feel compelled to talk about it. Once we have mentioned triteness and forced rhythm, albeit the honest expression of a common feeling, nothing remains to be said about the poem "Morning." And reference to the history of production of inferior works of art does not add much. Few works are as open to completely divergent interpretations as in *The Turn of the Screw*. There are some, of course—*Hamlet*, the *Mona Lisa*, *Paradise Lost*. We can puzzle, too, over how to interpret great paintings. Frank Cioffi asks, "Is the Moses of Michelangelo about to hurl the tablets of the law to the ground or has he just overcome the impulse to do so?" and goes on to ask questions like these of other well-known works: Tennyson's *In Memoriam*, Keats's "Ode on a Grecian Urn," Pope's *Sporus*, Wordsworth's *Ode*, Shakespeare's *Othello* and Sonnet 73, Yeats's "Among School Children," Ford Madox Ford's *Parade's End*, Eliot's "East Coker" and "A Cooking Egg," Dickens's *The Mystery of Edwin Drood*, James's *The Turn of the Screw*, *The Ambassadors*, and *The Golden Bowl*.[56]

But what can we ask about Rockwell's painting? It is difficult to ask or say interesting things when everything is apparent; the pleasures accompanying decoding are missing. In a sense, all good works of art are like a mystery novel. The pleasure comes from being given clues, not just the solution itself. This is why sophisticated viewers are apt to find *The Waste Land* more satisfying than "Morning." We do not tire of looking at Vermeer as quickly as we do of looking at Rockwell. Furthermore, we are eager to hear what others have to say about Vermeer, eager to hear how and with whom he can be compared. With Rockwell we have very little, if any, drive to hear what others have to say about it.

Evaluation can, of course, often be made on the basis of the presence or absence of evidence of craftsmanship, or on the basis of formal properties, without recourse to extrinsic properties. All I need to do is look at the cardinal birdbath (see plate VII). I see immediately that it is bad. The colors of the bird are too gross and gaudy and garish. The bird does not balance with the base. The cardinals and cherubs do not go well together. These remarks are appropriate, however, only to a discussion of the object as a work of art. They are legitimate if the gardener has placed it in the yard with an invitation that it be discussed in these terms, that is, in ways traditionally identified as aesthetic. If the gardener objects that gaudy colors attract more and rarer birds and that's why it is there, we can still call attention to the lack of proportion and gaudiness, but we can no longer fault the gardener's taste, or inability to distinguish art from nonart.

We are now ready to answer the question, How can there be bad art? First of all, we must recognize that even with things typically considered bad (or mediocre) we often find that information concerning history of production calls attention to some properties worth attending to. Our definition of art thus does not exclude mediocre works. One summer some colleagues and I spent several evenings looking and talking about slides. When I showed some Rockwell slides, a howl went up—but nevertheless we still found things to say. Upon hearing that Rockwell was influenced by Vermeer, we looked for signs of influence; we were surprised with how much we found.

But we can solve the problem of how an object with apparently no redeeming properties at all can still qualify as a 'work of art' in another way as well. As we saw in chapter 4, there are properties of a kind generally considered worth attending to. The term 'work of art' is often used in ways analogous to the use of the word 'wine'. What does one who says, "They didn't serve wine, they served Mogen David," mean? Not, literally, that wine was not served. After all, don't we purchase Mogen David in the wine section of a liquor store? Doesn't it fall under all of the laws regulating the sale and use of wine? It has the kind of properties generally attributed to wine: it comes from grapes, it is a liquid, it has a certain alcoholic content, it tastes fruity, and it smells fruity. Even if it's not *worth* drinking, it is still wine.[57]

Likewise, artifacts that are not worth attending to can still be works of art if information concerning their history of production calls attention to the *sort* of property generally considered worth attending to: color, shape, rhyme scheme, harmony, structure of elements—all of the things we consider under the vague term "aesthetic properties."

Mogen David has bouquet; it can hence be distinguished from, say, water. But it doesn't have a very interesting bouquet, and perhaps, even, has a distasteful one. Similarly, the on-velvet depiction of the Arc de Triomphe (see plate VI) has shapes and colors and decorative intent. But there is no complexity or richness in the ways the properties are presented. The properties are simply not very interesting; we might even say they are revolting. What distinguishes Reynolds's *Strawberry Girl* from the paintings of the Keanes and Lees obviously is not the content per se (though I think Keane does Reynolds some disservice on this score) but rests in the fact that critics have been moved to talk about Reynolds and not the Keanes. One might find it difficult to convince the fans of the Keanes that their paintings do not "reveal universal human values" as Reynolds's portraits have been said to do.[58] But it is impossible to find critics attempting to fit the Keanes into important painterly traditions. Our perception of Reynolds's work is sharpened when we are told by Ellis Waterhouse that in spite of the fact that Reynolds accepted the prevailing view that Florentine draughtsmanship was superior to Venetian color,

> Reynolds' mastery lies essentially in the Venetian tradition, in colour, in chiaroscuro, in the arrangement of masses in which the outlines are never hard. His feeling for placing of a figure within the confines of a frame is never at fault, and his control of the pattern of light and shade over the whole area is equally masterly.[59]

The burden of finding equally interesting things to say about the Keanes' work lies with their supporters.

The normative nature of the term 'work of art' thus follows, as Søren Kjørup has suggested, from the fact that to so dub an object "is to commit the object to a very special sort of treatment to which a lot of value is attached, partly because it is the treatment characteristically given to very valuable objects. To say that something is a work of art even in the classificatory way is to say that the object, although it may be a *bad* work of art, is still one of the things that should normally be evaluated in a certain way."[60] The special treatment these objects are given consists of discussing them in certain ways, and with a specialized vocabulary. This vocabulary is found in the history, criticism and theory of art. The terms of the vocabulary refer to properties that have generally, historically, traditionally been thought to bear attending to. I hold up an object and claim that it is a work of art because it has some of those properties, and when I tell you about their history you will be able to perceive them.

Tastes, even traditions, change. We find different ways of describing things in different times and places. Not only do the intrinsic properties considered important vary; so also do the extrinsic ones. We also look for new things, sometimes by choice, sometimes because artists force us to. Influenced by those who go before, artists to a great extent determine which are the properties worth attending to. If artists in large numbers began copying Rockwell's style, we would probably experience a critical reassessment of his work. But artists also operate within various contexts and institutions, social, political, and philosophical. All of these factors bear upon the ways in which their products will be discussed, and this in turn determines which products are works of art.

So what about the orange crate and the moose call? The group in our original garden cannot settle their argument simply by looking more closely at the objects before them. They must first find out if what they are perceiving is an artifact—the easiest part of their task by far. The greater part of their task concerns the ways in which each of the objects has been, is, or will be, discussed. Does information regarding its history of production lead one to focus on properties generally considered worth attending to that might not have been looked at before? If both the crucial history and the crucial properties are there, present in both orange crates, there are two works of art. If in only one, there is only one work of art. If in neither, there are no works of art. If Roberta Peters utters a moose call in her concert tonight, has she sung a song? Perhaps we'll have to wait for tomorrow's review to find out.

Notes

Chapter 1

1. Morris Weitz, "The Role of Theory in Aesthetics," *Journal of Aesthetics and Art Criticism* 15 (1956): 31.

2. Ibid.,p. 32.

3. Hilton Kramer, "The Emperor's New Bikini," *Art in America* 57 (January 1969): 49–50.

4. We could, perhaps, imagine situations in which the observer was quite correct. The doctors are fiends playing an elaborate game of "Button, button, who's got the button." But in my example it is serious surgery that is being performed.

5. Weitz, "Role of Theory," p. 30.

6. Mario de Micheli *Cézanne* (London: Thames and Hudson, Dolphin Books, 1968), p. 19.

7. Teddy Brunius, *Theory and Taste* (Uppsala Universitetet, Stockholm: Almqvist & Wiksell, 1969), p. 105.

8. Edward Bullough, " 'Psychical Distance' as a Factor in Art and an Esthetic Principle," in *A Modern Book of Esthetics*, 3rd ed., ed. Melvin Rader (New York: Holt, Rinehart and Winston, 1960), p. 395.

9. Ibid., pp. 395–96.

10. José Ortega y Gasset, "The Dehumanization of Art," in *A Modern Book of Esthetics*, 3rd ed., ed. Melvin Rader (New York: Holt, Rinehart and Winston, 1960), p. 415.

11. Roger Fry, "The Artist and Psychoanalysis," in *The Hogarth Essays*, ed. Leonard S. Woolf and Virginia S. Woolf (1924; reprinted, Freeport, N.Y.: Books for Libraries Press Reprint Series, 1970), p. 297.

12. George Dickie, "The Myth of the Aesthetic Attitude," *American Philosophical Quarterly* 1 (1964): 56–65.

13. Fry, "Artist and Psychoanalysis," pp. 297–98.

14. Edmund Burke, *A Philosophical Enquiry into the Origin of Our Ideas of the Sublime and Beautiful* (1759; facsimile of copy in Yale University Library, New York: Garland Publishing, 1971).

Chapter 2

1. Teddy Brunius, "Theory and Ideologies in Art," in *Culture and Art*, ed. Lars Aagard-Mogensen (Nyborg: F. Lokkes Forlag and Atlantic Highlands, N.J.: Humanities Press, 1976), p. 69.

2. Teddy Brunius, *Theory and Taste* (Uppsala University, Stockholm: Almqvist and Wiksell, 1969), p. 16.

159

3. Søren Kjørup, "Art Broadly and Wholly Conceived," in *Culture and Art*, ed. Lars Aagard-Mogensen (Nyborg: F. Lokkes Forlag and Atlantic Highlands, N.J.: Humanities Press, 1976), p. 47.

4. This is the version of the poem used by Rosenthal and Smith. (See note 5.)

5. M. L. Rosenthal and A. J. M. Smith, *Exploring Poetry* (New York: Macmillan Co., 1955), pp. 69–70.

6. Lorenz Eitner, *Géricault's "Raft of the Medusa"* (London: Phaidon Press, 1972), p. 41.

7. Bernhard Berenson, *The Italian Painters of the Renaissance* (London: Clarendon Press, 1930), p. 65.

8. E. H. Gombrich, "Art and Scholarship," in *Meditations on a Hobby Horse*, 2nd ed. (London: Phaidon Press, 1963), p. 11.

9. Deryck Cooke, *The Language of Music* (Oxford: Oxford University Press, 1959), p. 156.

10. Berenson, *Italian Painters*, pp. 1–58.

11. Bernhard Berenson, "Preface" to *Italian Painters of the Renaissance* (London: Phaidon, 1952), p. xii.

12. Constantine Leontiev, "The Greatness of *War and Peace*," in *The Norton Critical Edition of "War and Peace,"* ed. George Gibian (New York: W. W. Norton and Co., 1966), p. 1390.

13. Ibid.

14. C. J. Ducasse, *Art, the Critics, and You* (New York: Liberal Arts Press, 1944), p. 116.

15. Arnold Isenberg, "Critical Communication," *Philosophical Review* 58, no. 4 (1949): pp. 330–44.

16. Ibid., p. 336.

17. Paul Ziff, "Reasons in Art Criticism," in *Philosophy and Education*, ed. Israel Scheffler (Boston: Allyn and Bacon, 1958), pp. 219–36.

18. Kenneth Clark, *Looking at Pictures* (London: John Murray, 1960), p. 37.

19. Maria Shirley, "Hapsburg Patronage and the Influence of Italy," in *Art Treasures in Spain*, ed. Bernard S. Myers and Trevin Copplestone (New York and London: McGraw-Hill, 1969), p. 85.

20. Bernard Berenson, *Italian Painters* (Clarendon edition), pp. 63–64.

21. Bernard Ashmole, *Architect and Sculptor in Classical Greece* (London: Phaidon Press, 1972), pp. 6–7.

22. Rudolf Arnheim, *Art and Visual Perception* (Berkeley, Calif.: University of California Press, 1954), p. 21.

23. Michael Fried, "Art and Objecthood," *Artforum* 6 (Summer 1967):15.

24. Guido Ballo, *The Critical Eye: A New Approach to Art Appreciation*, trans. R. H. Boothroyd (London: Heinemann, 1969), pp. 112–13.

25. David Cecil, *Hardy the Novelist* (London: Constable & Co., 1943), p. 20.

26. Viggo Kjaer Peterson, Program notes to Danish Royal Ballet's 1978 production of *Den forunderlinge Mandarin*, translated by the author.

27. Ballo, *Critical Eye*, p. 114.

28. Shirley, "Hapsburg Patronage," p. 78.

29. Kenneth Clark, *Looking at Pictures*, p. 124.

30. Shirley, "Hapsburg Patronage," p. 85.

31. E. H. Gombrich, "Tradition and Expression in Western Still Life," in *Meditations on a Hobby Horse*, 2nd ed. (London: Phaidon Press, 1963), p. 99.

32. Berenson, *Italian Painters* (Clarendon edition), p. 36.

33. T. S. Eliot, "Tradition and the Individual Talent," in *Selected Essays, 1919* (London: Faber & Faber, 1919), pp. 3–11.

34. Jean Christophe Ammann, "Arms and Legs: Five Danish Artists in Kunstmuseum Luzern: Comments on Some Works," *North-Information* no. 5–6 (1977), pp. 11–12.

35. René Wellek and Austin Warren, *Theory of Literature* (New York: Harcourt Brace & Co., 1956), p. 67.

36. Shirley, "Hapsburg Patronage," p. 78.

37. Ernest Jones, "The Death of Hamlet's Father," in *Essays in Applied Psychoanalysis* (London: Hogarth Press, 1964), p. 323.

38. C. S. Lewis, "Psycho-analysis and Literary Criticism," in *Selected Literary Essays*, ed. Walter Hooper (Cambridge: Cambridge University Press, 1969), p. 286.

39. Ernest Jones, "The Problem of Paul Morphy," in *Essays in Applied Psychoanalysis* (London: Hogarth Press, 1951), p. 194.

40. See Richard Wollheim, ed., *Freud, A Collection of Critical Essays* (New York: Anchor Books, Doubleday, 1974). Of particular interest in this regard are the essays by Wesley Salmon and Clark Glymour.

41. Ludwig Wittgenstein, *Lectures and Conversations on Aesthetics, Psychology, and Religious Belief* (Berkeley, Calif.: University of California Press, 1972), p. 44.

42. Ibid., p. 50.

43. Clark, *Looking at Pictures*, p. 34.

44. Tom Burns Haber, *A. E. Housman* (New York: Twayne Publishers, 1967), p. 76.

45. Arnheim, *Art and Visual Perception*, pp. 84–85.

46. Irving Sandler, *The Triumph of American Painting: A History of Abstract Expressionism* (New York: Praeger, 1970), p. 1.

47. Marcia Eaton, "Art, Artifacts and Intentions," *American Philosophical Quarterly* 6, no. 2 (April 1969): 165–69.

48. Adrian Stokes, *The Image in Form, Selected Writings of Adrian Stokes*, ed. Richard Wollheim (New York: Icon Editions, Harper and Row, 1972), p. 43.

49. Ananda Coomaraswamy, *Figures of Speech or Figures of Thought* (London: Luzac & Co., 1946), p. 124.

50. W. K. Wimsatt and Monroe C. Beardsley, "The Intentional Fallacy," in *The Verbal Icon* (Lexington, Ky.: University of Kentucky Press, 1954), p. 4.

51. Ibid., p. 11.

52. W. K. Wimsatt, "History and Criticism," in *The Verbal Icon*, pp. 262–63.

53. Vachel Lindsay, "The Eagle That is Forgotten," in *The Mentor Book of Major American Poets*, ed. Oscar Williams and Edwin Honig (New York: Mentor Books, 1962), p. 257.

54. Immanuel Kant, *Critique of Judgment*, trans. J. H. Bernard, London, 1892 (New York: Hafner Library of Classics, 1963), p. 183.

55. John Dewey, *Art as Experience* (New York: Mimton Balch & Co., 1934), p. 48.

56. Richard Benedict, "The Alhambra," in *Art Treasures in Spain*, ed. Bernard S. Myers and Trevin Copplestone (New York and London: McGraw-Hill, 1969), p. 57.

57. Sandler, *The Triumph of American Painting*, p. 56.

58. F. R. Leavis, *The Great Tradition* (London: Chatto and Windus, 1973), pp. 92–93.

59. A. Walton Litz, "Into the Nineteenth Century," in *Jane Austen: A Study of Her Artistic Development* (New York: Oxford University Press, 1965), pp. 100–101.

60. Cooke, *The Language of Music*, p. 159.

61. Ibid., p. 162.

62. Desmond Collins, "Stone Age Hunters, Iberians, and Romans," in *Art Treasures in Spain*, ed. Myers and Copplestone, p. 9.

63. Clark, *Looking at Pictures*, p. 64.

64. Mary McCarthy, Review of *Pale Fire*, by Vladimir Nabokov, *New Republic*, June 1962, pp. 21–27.

65. Andrew Field, *Nabokov, His Life in Art* (Boston and Toronto: Little, Brown & Co., 1967), p. 299.

66. Jones, *Essays in Applied Psychonalysis* p. 324.

67. Ibid., p. 35.

68. E. H. Gombrich, "Psycho-Analysis and the History of Art," in *Meditations on a Hobby Horse*, p. 32.

69. Longinus, *On the Sublime*, trans. William Smith, 2nd ed. (London: W. Sandby, 1742).

70. In particular, see John Ruskin, *Modern Painters*, vol. 2 (New York: C. E. Merrill and Co., 1891).

71. Leo Tolstoy, *What Is Art?* (1896; reprint ed., New York: Bobbs-Merrill, 1960).

72. It is not always clear with Tolstoy (as with others) whether he is separating art from nonart or good art from bad art. We shall here deal with his remarks as if they were intended to shed light on the first distinction. The relation of subject matter to the distinction between good and bad art will be dealt with in chapter 5.

73. Harold Osborne, *Aesthetics and Art Theory: An Historical Introduction* (London: Harlow, Longmans Green, & Co. 1968), p. 6.

74. See for example, D. W. Gotshalk, *Art and the Social Order* (New York: Dover, 1962). He identifies functional theories as one of four main theories of art; the other three are the genetic, formal, and expressionist.

75. Ballo, *Critical Eye*, p. 195.

76. Annette Rubenstein, *The Great Tradition in English Literature from Shakespeare to Shaw*, 2 vols. (New York and London: Modern Reader Paperbacks, 1953), 2:703.

77. Sandler, *Triumph of American Art*, p. 8.

78. I. A. Richards, "Art, Play, and Civilization," in *Principles of Literary Criticism* New York: Harcourt Brace & World, Inc. A Harvest Book, (first published, 1925), p. 228.

79. Tolstoy, *What Is Art?* p. 51.

80. Edmund Wilson, "Marxism and Literature," *Atlantic Monthly*, December 1937, p. 748.

81. Wellek and Warren, *Theory of Literature*, p. 37.

82. Melvin Rader and Bertram Jessup, *Art and Human Values* (Englewood Cliffs, N.J.: Prentice-Hall. 1976), p. 132.

83. Leroi Jones, *Black Music* (New York: William Morrow & Co., 1967), p. 14.

84. Brunius, *Theory and Taste*, p. 25.

85. Ballo, *Critical Eye*, p. 104.

86. Ibid., p. 120.

87. Berenson, *Italian Painters* (Clarendon edition), pp. 34–35.

88. Ibid., pp. 11–13.

89. Arnold Kettle, *An Introduction to the English Novel* (London: Hutchinson University Library, 1951), pp. 83–84.

90. Collins, "Stone Age Hunters," p. 10.

91. Mary Orr, "The Dark Ages and the Rise of the Caliphates," in *Art Treasures in Spain*, p. 9.

92. See *The Sociology of Art and Literture*, ed. Milton Albrecht, James H. Bennett, and Mason Griff (London: Duckworth and Co., 1970).

93. Milton Albrecht, "Art as an Institution," *American Sociological Review* 33 (1968): 386.

94. Lucien Goldmann, "The Sociology of Literature: Status and Problems of Method," *International Social Science Journal* 19, no. 4 (1967): 496.

95. Ibid, p. 505.

96. Ibid., pp. 505–6.

97. Wellek and Warren, *Theory of Literature*, p. 102.

98. Edmund Wilson, *Marxism and Literature*, p. 747.

99. Ibid., p. 747.

100. Arthur C. Danto, "The Artworld," *Journal of Philosophy* 61 (1964).

101. George Dickie, *Art and Aesthetic: An Institutional Analysis* (Ithaca, N.Y. and London: Cornell University Press, 1974), p. 34.

102. Ibid., p. 49.

103. Ibid., p. 37.

104. Monroe C. Beardsley, "Is Art Essentially Institutional?" in *Culture and Art*, ed. Lars Aagard-Mogensen (Atlantic Highlands, N.J.: Humanities Press, 1976), p. 199.

105. Ted Cohen, "The Possibility of Art: Remarks on a Proposal by Dickie," *Philosophical Review* 82 (January 1973): 69–82.

106. Ibid., p. 71.

107. Ibid., p. 72.

108. Ibid., p. 73.

109. The remainder of Cohen's article deals with an interesting suggestion that conferral of candidacy is a complex speech-act. As will be seen later, I believe that speech-acts are part of what makes art art, but I do not think it is possible to capture the essential nature of art in terms of a single type of such action.

110. Joseph Margolis, "Works of Art are Physically Embodied and Culturally Emergent Entities," *British Journal of Aesthetics* 74 (1974): 190.

111. Ibid., pp. 192–93.

112. Ibid., p. 187.

113. Beardsley, "Is Art Essentially Institutional?" p. 207.

114. John M. Ellis, *The Theory of Literary Criticism: A Logical Analysis* (Berkeley, Calif.: University of California Press, 1974), p. 31.

115. Ibid., p. 44.

116. Ibid., p. 48.

Chapter 3

1. The essentialist-nominalist argument is not important here. While preferring predicate- or label-talk myself, I see no reason that one must adopt it in order to understand and accept this discussion.

2. Arthur Danto, "The Transfiguration of the Commonplace," *Journal of Aesthetics and Art Criticism* 35, no. 2 (Winter 1974): 138–48.

3. Ibid., p. 140.

4. For their discussions on this point, see Nelson Goodman, *The Languages of Art* (Indianapolis and New York: Bobbs-Merrill, 1968), and E. H. Gombrich, *Art and Illusion* (New York: Pantheon Books, Random House, 1960).

5. Danto, "Transfiguration," p. 143.

6. Oscar Cargill, *The Novels of Henry James* (New York: Macmillan Co., 1961), p. 385.

7. Walter Havighurst, *Voices on the River: The Story of the Mississippi Waterways* (New York: Macmillan Co., 1964), p. 83.

8. Robert Edgar Riegel, *The Story of the Western Railroads* (Gloucester, Mass.: Peter Smith, 1974), pp. 263–64.

9. "Indentations in Space," *New Yorker*, 21 November 1977, p. 52.

10. Ibid., p. 51.

11. Goodman, *The Languages of Art*, pp. 99–123.

Chapter 4

1. For these and other interpretations of James's novel, see Henry James, *The Turn of the Screw*, ed. Robert Kimbrough (New York: W. W. Norton & Co., 1966).

2. Marcia Eaton, "Art, Artifacts and Intentions," *American Philosophical Quarterly* 6, no. 2 (1969): 165–69.

3. Henry David Aiken, "The Aesthetic Relevance of Artists' Intentions," *Journal of Philosophy* 52 (1955): 742–53.

4. J. L. Austin, *How to Do Things with Words*, ed. J. O. Urmson (Cambridge, Mass.: Harvard, 1962).

5. John Searle, *Speech Acts: An Essay in the Philosophy of Language* (London: Cambridge University Press, 1969).

6. Lewis Carroll, *Collected Verse* (New York: E. P. Dutton & Co., 1929), pp. 125–29.

7. For a discussion of the kinds of things that can be done with pictures, see Søren Kjørup, "George Inness and 'The Battle of Hastings': Doing Things with Pictures," *Monist* 58 (April 1974): 216–35.

8. See Nelson Goodman's *Languages of Art* for a fuller discussion of this point (New York: Bobbs-Merrill, 1968).

9. I am grateful to my colleague Rolf Sartorius for making this point.

10. Carl R. Baldwin, "Art & Law: Property Right vs. 'Moral Right'," *Art in America* 62 (1974): 34.

11. George Kubler, *The Shape of Time: Remarks on the History of Things* (New Haven, Conn., and London: Yale University Press, 1962), p. 1.

12. J. O. Urmson, "What Makes a Situation Aesthetic?" *Proceedings of the Aristotelian Society* Supplementary Volume 31 (1975) 75–92.

13. Teddy Brunius, "Theories and Ideologies in Aesthetics," in *Culture and Art*, ed. Lars Aagard-Mogensen (Atlantic Highlands, N.J.: Humanities Press, 1976), p. 73.

14. Ibid., p. 70.

15. Kenneth Clark, *Looking at Pictures* (London: John Murray, 1960), pp. 16–17.

16. Lorenz Eitner, *Géricault's "Raft of the Medusa"* (London: Phaidon, 1972), p. 41.

17. David Hume, "Of the Standard of Taste," in *Four Dissertations* (1757; facsimile ed., New York: Garland Publishing, 1970), p. 232.

18. Washington Irving, *The Alhambra*, rev. ed. (New York: G. P. Putnam's Sons, 1865), pp. 66–67.

19. Ibid., pp. 64–65.

20. E. M. Forster, *Aspects of the Novel* (New York: Harcourt, Brace & Co., 1927), p. 28.

21. Frank Sibley, "Aesthetic and Nonaesthetic," *Philosophical Review* 74, no. 2 (April 1965): 135–59.

22. Douglas Davis, "Uses of Enchantment," *Newsweek*, 7 July 1980, p. 60.

23. Jerome Stolnitz, "'Beauty': Some Stages in the History of an Idea," *Journal of the History of Ideas* 22 (1961):185.

24. Davis, "Uses of Enchantment," p. 61.

25. P. F. Strawson, "Aesthetic Appraisal and Works of Art," in *Freedom and Resentment* (London: Methuen & Co., 1974), p. 180.

26. Walter Cahn, *Masterpieces: Chapters on the History of an Idea*, (Princeton, N.J.: Princeton University Press, 1979), p. 86.

27. Nelson Goodman, "When Is Art?" in *Ways of Worldmaking* (Indianapolis, Ind., and Cambridge: Hackett, 1978).

28. Rudolf Arnheim, *Art and Visual Perception* (Berkeley, Calif.: University of California Press, 1954), pp. 1–31.

29. Jack A. Hobbs, *Art in Context* (New York: Harcourt, Brace & World, 1975), p. 15.

30. Henry Adams, *The Education of Henry Adams* (New York: Modern Library, 1931), p. 380.

31. See Nelson Goodman, *The Languages of Art*.

32. Alan Tormey, "Aesthetic Rights," *Journal of Aesthetics and Art Criticism* 32 (Winter 1973); 163–70.

33. This point sheds some light on ontological problems of art—where and what is *the* work of art? It seems to be a single physical object in the case of paintings, a class of them in the case of novels and musical scores. The sense of loss I refer to is only felt when *all* members of the class have been destroyed.

34. "The Art of Grantsmanship in the U.S.," *International Herald Tribune*, 29 May 1978, p. 16.

35. "Indentations in Space," *New Yorker*, 21 November 1977, p. 51.

36. David Hume, "Of the Standard of Taste," p. 232.

37. Morris Weitz, "The Role of Theory in Aesthetics," *Journal of Aesthetics and Art Criticism* 15, no. 1 (September 1956): 27–35.

Chapter 5

1. Guido Ballo, *The Critical Eye: A New Approach to Art Appreciation*, trans. R. H. Boothroyd (London: Heinemann, 1969), p. 44.

2. Ibid., p. 139.

3. "Instant Late Show," *Time*, 22 August 1977, p. 56.

4. Northrop Frye, *Anatomy of Criticism* (Princeton, N.J.: Princeton University Press, 1957), p. 17.

5. *Newsweek*, 2 March 1964, p. 54.

6. Lorenz Eitner, *Géricault's "Raft of the Medusa"* (London: Phaidon, 1972), pp. 4–5.

7. Ballo, *Critical Eye*, p. 243.

8. Donald Jay Grout, *A History of Western Music* (New York: W. W. Norton & Co., 1960), p. 282.

9. C. S. Lewis, "Psycho-Analysis and Literary Criticism," in *Selected Literary Essays*, ed. Walter Hooper (Cambridge: Cambridge University Press, 1969), p. 314.

10. *Newsweek*, 21 November 1977.

11. David Hume, "Of the Standard of Taste," in *Four Dissertations* (1757), facsimile edition (New York: Garland Publishing, 1970).

12. See Hume, "Standard of Taste," and Francis Hutcheson, "Essay on the Nature and Conduct of the Passions and Affections, with Illustrations of the Moral Sense" (1728), in *Four Dissertations* (Garland edition).

13. Hume, "Standard of Taste," p. 232.

14. C. S. Lewis, "High Brows and Low Brows," in *Rehabilitations and Other Essays* (London: Oxford University Press, 1939), p. 101.

15. E. H. Gombrich, "Visual Metaphors of Value in Art," in *Meditations on a Hobby Horse*, 2nd ed. (London and New York: Phaidon, 1971), p. 18.

16. Ballo, *Critical Eye*, p. 44.

17. E. M. Forster, *Aspects of the Novel* (New York: Harcourt, Brace & Co., 1927), p. 109.

18. I. A. Richards, "Badness in Poetry," in *Principles of Literary Criticism* (New York: Harcourt, Brace & Co., 1925), p. 199.

19. Ibid., p. 200.

20. Ibid., p. 202.

21. Ibid., p. 203.

22. Ibid., p. 205.

23. Ibid., p. 204.

24. In the following remarks I am greatly indebted to a student of mine, Ms. Terri Alwell. My discussions with her and a paper she submitted to me, "A Study of the Influence of Jan Vermeer of Delft on the works of Norman Rockwell," were invaluable.

25. Norman Rockwell, *My Adventures as an Illustrator: As Told to Thomas Rockwell* (New York: Doubleday and Co., 1960), p. 86.

26. Classroom experience leads me to believe that there will be someone among my readers who says, at this point, "He isn't." I can only hope that the reader's opinion will be changed by the end of this chapter.

27. Arnheim, *Art and Visual Perception* (Berkeley, Calif.: University of California Press, 1954), p. 32.

28. Ballo, *Critical Eye*, p. 56.

29. James Edward Holroyd, "Whit about McGonagall?" *In Britain*, June 1978, p. 12.

30. Terri Alwell, "A Study of the Influence of Jan Vermeer of Delft on the Works of Norman Rockwell," unpublished, pp. 4–5.

31. Dorothy Canfield Fisher, Preface to *Norman Rockwell Illustrator*, by Arthur L. Guptill (New York: Ballantine Books, 1946), p. viii.

32. Ibid.

33. Ibid., p. ix.

34. Arthur L. Guptill, *Norman Rockwell Illustrator* (New York: Ballantine Books, 1946), p. xxi.

35. Irving Sandler, *The Triumph of American Art* (New York and Washington, D.C.: Praeger, 1970), p. 11.

36. F. R. Leavis, *The Great Tradition* (London: Chatto and Windus, 1973), p. 30.

37. Quoted in Guptill, *Norman Rockwell Illustrator*, p. 53.

38. Helen Vendler, "The Demands of Poetry on Criticism," *Key Reporter* 43, no. 1 (Autumn 1977), p. 2.

39. Leavis, *The Great Tradition;* see especially chapter 1.

40. Gombrich, "Visual Metaphors," p. 20.

41. Guptill, *Norman Rockwell Illustrator*, p. 135.

42. Leavis, *The Great Tradition*, p. 19.

43. For a discussion of this and other cartoons, see E. H. Gombrich, "The Cartoonist's Armoury," in *Meditations on a Hobby Horse*, pp. 127–42.

44. Ibid., p. 131.

45. Lewis Carroll, *Collected Verse* (New York: E. P. Dutton & Co., 1929), pp. 125–29.

46. Arnheim, *Art and Visual Perception*, p. 45.

47. Sloan Wilson, *All the Best People* (London: Cassell, 1971), p. 494.

48. Ford Madox Ford, *The Good Soldier*, The Bodley Head Ford Madox Ford, Vol. 1, ed. Graham Greene (London: The Bodley Head, 1962), p. 75.

49. Ibid., p. 1.

50. E. H. Gombrich, *Art and Illusion* (New York: Pantheon Books, 1960), p. 385.

51. E. H. Gombrich, "Psycho-Analysis and the History of Art," in *Meditations on a Hobby Horse*, p. 37.

52. Jerry Williams, in *Young America Sings*, ed. Dennis Hartman (Los Angeles, Calif.: National High School Poetry Association, 1955), p. 79.

53. Gombrich, *Art and Illusion*, p. 313.

54. For an anthology of the main critical writings see Henry James, *The Turn of the Screw*, ed. Robert Kimbrough, Norton Critical Edition (New York: W. W. Norton & Co., 1966).

55. Harold C. Goddard, "A Pre-Freudian Reading of *The Turn of the Screw*," in *Nineteenth-Century Fiction* 12 (June 1957): 3–4; reprinted in Norton Critical edition, pp. 183–84.

56. Frank Cioffi, "Intention and Interpretation in Criticism," *Proceedings of the Aristotelian Society*, Supplementary Volume, 64 (1963–64): 85–87.

57. I am indebted to Allan Buchanan and Michael Root for this comparison.

58. Ellis Waterhouse, *Reynolds* (London: Phaidon, 1973), p. 9.

59. Ibid., p. 11.

60. Søren Kjørup, "Art Broadly and Wholly Conceived," in *Culture and Art*, ed. Lars Aagard- Mogensen (Nyborg: F. Løkkes Forlag and Atlantic Highlands, N.J.: Humanities Press, 1976), p. 51.

Bibliography

Adams, Henry. *The Education of Henry Adams*. New York: Modern Library, 1931.

Aiken, Henry David. "The Aesthetic Relevance of Artists' Intentions." *Journal of Philosophy* 52 (1955). 742–753.

Albrecht, Milton. "Art as an Institution." *American Sociological Review* 33 (1968). 383–397.

————; Bennett, James H.; and Griff, Mason, eds. *The Sociology of Art and Literature*. London: Duckworth and Co., 1970.

Ammann, Jean Christophe. "Arms and Legs: Five Danish Artists in Kunstmuseum Luzern: Comments on Some Works." *North-Information* nos. 5–6 (1977): 11–12.

Arnheim, Rudolf. *Art and Visual Perception*. Berkeley, Calif.: University of California Press, 1954.

Ashmole, Bernard. *Architect and Sculptor in Classical Greece*. London: Phaidon Press, 1972.

Austin, J. L. *How to Do Things with Words*. Edited by J. O. Urmson. Cambridge, Mass.: Harvard University Press, 1962.

Baldwin, Carl R. "Art & Law: Property Right vs. 'Moral Right'," *Art in America* 62 (1974): 20–22.

Ballo, Guido. *The Critical Eye, A New Approach to Art Appreciation*, Translated by R. H. Boothroyd. London: Heinemann, 1969.

Beardsley, Monroe C. "Is Art Essentially Institutional?" in *Culture and Art*, edited by Lars Aagard-Mogensen. Atlantic Highlands, N.J.: Humantities Press, 1976.

Berenson, Bernhard. *The Italian Painters of the Renaissance*. London: Clarendon Press, 1930.

Brunius, Teddy.*Theory and Taste*. Uppsala Universitetet, Stockholm: Almqvist & Wiksell, 1969.

Bullough, Edward. "'Psychical Distance' as a Factor in Art and an Esthetic Principle." In *A Book of Modern Esthetics*, 3rd ed., edited by Melvin Rader. New York: Holt, Rinehart & Winston, 1960.

Burke, Edmund. *A Philosophical Enquiry into the Origin of our Ideas of the Sublime and Beautiful*. 1759. Facsimile of copy in Yale University Library. New York: Garland Publishing, 1971.

Cahn, Walter. *Masterpieces: Chapters on the History of an Idea*. Princeton, N.J.: Princeton University Press, 1979.

Cargill, Oscar. *The Novels of Henry James*. New York: Macmillan Co., 1961.

Carroll, Lewis. *Collected Verse*. New York: E. P. Dutton & Co., 1929.

Cecil, David. *Hardy the Novelist*. London: Constable & Co., 1943.

Cioffi, Frank, "Intention and Interpretation in Criticism." *Proceedings of the Aristotelian Society*, Supplementary Volume, 64 (1963–64).

Clark, Kenneth. *Looking at Pictures*. London: John Murray, 1960.

Cohen, Ted. "The Possibility of Art: Remarks on a Proposal by Dickie." *Philosophical Review* 82 (January 1973): 69–82.

Cooke, Deryck. *The Language of Music*. Oxford: Oxford University Press, 1959.

Coomaraswamy, Ananda. *Figures of Speech or Figures of Thought*. London: Luzak & Co., 1946.

Danto, Arthur C. "The Artworld." *Journal of Philosophy* 61 (1964): 571–584.

———. "The Transfiguration of the Commonplace." *Journal of Aesthetics and Art Criticism* 35, no. 2 (Winter 1974): 138–148.

de Micheli, Mario. *Cézanne*. London: Thames and Hudson, Dolphin Books, 1968.

Dewey, John. *Art as Experience*. New York: Minton Balch & Co., 1934.

Dickie, George. *Art and the Aesthetic: An Institutional Analysis*. Ithaca, N.Y., and London: Cornell University Press, 1974.

———. "The Myth of the Aesthetic Attitude." *American Philosophical Quarterly* 1 (1964): 56–65

Ducasse, C. J. *Art, the Critics, and You*. New York: Liberal Arts Press, 1944.

Eaton, Marcia. "Art, Artifacts and Intentions." *American Philosophical Quarterly* 6, no. 2 (April 1969): 165–169

Eitner, Lorenz. *Géricault's "Raft of the Medusa."* London: Phaidon Press, 1972.

Eliot, T. S. "Tradition and the Individual Talent." In *Selected Essays, 1919*. London: Faber & Faber, 1919.

Ellis, John M.. *The Theory of Literary Criticism: A Logical Analysis* Berkeley, Calif.: University of California Press, 1974.

Field, Andrew. *Nabokov, His Life in Art*. Boston and Toronto: Little, Brown & Co., 1967.

Fisher, Dorothy Canfield. Preface to *Norman Rockwell Illustrator*, by Arthur L. Guptill. New York: Ballantine Books, 1946.

Ford, Ford Madox. *The Good Soldier*. The Bodley Head Ford Madox Ford, Vol. 1, edited by Graham Greene. (London: The Bodley Head, 1962; also New York: Alfred A. Knopf, 1951.

Forster, E. M. *Aspects of the Novel*. New York: Harcourt, Brace & Co., 1927.

Fried, Michael. "Art and Objecthood." *Artforum* 5 (Summer 1967): 12–23.

Fry, Roger. "The Artist and Psychoanalysis." In *The Hogarth Essays*, edited by Leonard S. Woolf and Virginia S. Woolf. 1924; reprinted, Freeport, N.Y.: Books for Libraries Press Reprint Series, 1970.

Frye, Northrop. *Anatomy of Criticism*. Princeton, N.J.: Princeton University Press, 1957.

Goddard, Harold C. "A Pre-Freudian Reading of '*The Turn of the Screw*.'" *Nineteenth Century Fiction* 12 (June 1957): 1–36.

Goldmann, Lucien, "The Sociology of Literature: Status and Problems of Method." *International Social Science Journal* 19, no. 4 (1967): 493–516.

Gombrich, E. H. *Art and Illusion*. New York: Pantheon Books, Random House, 1960.

———. *Meditations on a Hobby Horse*. London: Phaidon Press, 1963.

Goodman, Nelson. *The Languages of Art*. Indianapolis, Ind., and New York: Bobbs-Merrill, 1968.

———. "When is Art?" In *Ways of Worldmaking* (Indianapolis, Ind., and Cambridge: Hackett, 1978.

Gotshalk, D. W. *Art and the Social Order*. New York: Dover, 1962.

Grout, Donald Jay, *A History of Western Music*. New York: W. W. Norton & Co., 1960.

Guptill, Arthur L. *Norman Rockwell Illustrator*. New York: Ballantine Books, 1946.

Haber, Tom Burns. *A. E. Housman*. New York: Twayne Publishers, 1967.

Havighurst, Walter. *Voices on the River: The Story of the Mississippi Waterways*. New York: Macmillan Co., 1964.

Hobbs, Jack A. *Art in Context*. New York: Harcourt, Brace & World, 1975.

Holroyd, James Edward. "Whit aboot McGonagall?" *In Britain*, June 1978: 12–13.

Housman, A. E. *Collected Poems*. New York: Henry Holt & Co., 1940; also London: Johnathan Cape, 1962.

Hume, David. "Of the Standard of Taste." In *Four Dissertations*. 1757. Facsimile edition. New York: Garland Publishing, 1970.

Irving, Washington. *The Alhambra*. Rev. ed. New York: G. P. Putnam's Sons, 1865.

Isenberg, Arnold. "Critical Communication." *Philosophical Review* 58, no. 4 (1949): 330–344.

James, Henry. *The Turn of the Screw*. Edited by Robert Kimbrough. Norton Critical Edition. New York: W. W. Norton & Co., 1966.

Jones, Ernest. *Essays in Applied Psychoanalysis*. London: Hogarth Press, 1951; also New York: International Universities Press, 1964.

Jones, Leroi. *Black Music*. New York: William Morrow & Co., 1967.

Kant, Immanuel. *Critique of Judgment*. Translated by J. H. Bernard, London, 1892. Reprint. New York: Hafner Library of Classics, 1963.

Kettle, Arnold. *An Introduction to the English Novel*. London: Hutchinson University Library, 1951.

Kjørup, Søren. "Art Broadly and Wholly Conceived." in *Culture and Art*, edited by Lars Aagard-Mogensen. Nyborg: F. Lokkes Forlag and Atlantic Highlands, N.J.: Humanities Press, 1976.

———. "George Inness and 'The Battle of Hastings': Doing Things with Pictures." *Monist* 58 (April 1974): 216–235

Kramer, Hilton. "The Emperor's New Bikini." *Art in America* 57 January 1969: 48–55.

Kubler, George. *The Shape of Time: Remarks on the History of Things*. New Haven, Conn., and London: Yale University Press, 1962.

Leavis, F. R. *The Great Tradition*. New York: New York University Press, 1960: also London: Chatto and Windus, 1973.

Leontiev, Constantine. "The Greatness of *War and Peace*." In *The Norton Critical*

Edition of War and Peace, edited by George Gibian. New York: W. W. Norton and Co., 1966.

Lewis, C. S. "High Brows and Low Brows," In *Rehabilitations and Other Essays*. London: Oxford University Press, 1939.

————. "Psycho-Analysis and Literary Criticism." In *Selected Literary Essays*, edited by Walter Hooper. Cambridge: Cambridge University Press, 1969.

Lindsay, Vachel. "The Eagle That Is Forgotten." In *The Mentor Book of Major American Poets*, edited by Oscar Williams and Edwin Honig. New York: Mentor Books, 1962.

Litz, A. Walton. "Into the Nineteenth Century." In *Jane Austen: A Study of Her Artistic Development*. New York: Oxford University Press, 1965.

Longinus. *On the Sublime*. Translated by William Smith. 2nd ed. London: W. Sandby, 1742.

McCarthy, Mary. Review of *Pale Fire*, by Vladimir Nabokov. *New Republic*, June 1962. 21–27.

Margolis, Joseph. "Works of Art Are Physically Embodied and Culturally Emergent Entities." *British Journal of Aesthetics* 74 (1974):187–196.

Myers, Bernard, and Copplestone, Trevin. *Art Treasures in Spain*. New York and London: McGraw-Hill, 1969.

Ortega y Gasset, José. "The Dehumanization of Art." In *A Modern Book of Esthetics*, 3rd ed., edited by Melvin Rader. New York: Holt, Rinehart & Winston, 1960.

Osborne, Harold. *Aesthetics and Art Theory: An Historical Introduction*. (London: Harlow, Longmans, Green, & Co., 1968).

Rader, Melvin, and Jessup, Bertram. *Art and Human Values*. Englewood Cliffs, N.J.: Prentice-Hall, 1976.

Richards, I. A., *Principles of Literary Criticism*. New York: Harcourt, Brace & Co., 1925; also London: Kegan, 1926.

Riegel, Robert Edgar. *The Story of the Western Railroads*. Gloucester, Mass.: Peter Smith, 1974.

Rockwell, Norman. *My Adventures as an Illustrator: As Told to Thomas Rockwell*. New York: Doubleday and Co., 1960.

Rosenthal, M. L., and Smith, A. J. M., *Exploring Poetry*. New York: Macmillan Co., 1955.

Rubenstein, Annette, *The Great Tradition in English Literature from Shakespeare to Shaw*. Vol. 2. New York and London: Modern Reader Paperbacks, 1953.

Ruskin, John. *Modern Painters*. Vol. 2. New York: C. E. Merrill and Co., 1891.

Sandler, Irving. *The Triumph of American Art*. New York and Washington, D.C.: Praeger, 1970.

Searle, John. *Speech Acts: An Essay in the Philosophy of Language*. London: Cambridge University Press, 1969.

Sibley, Frank. "Aesthetic and Nonaesthetic." *Philosophical Review* 74, no. 2 (April 1965):135–159.

Stokes, Adrian. *The Image in Form, Selected Writings of Adrian Stokes*. Edited by Richard Wollheim. New York: Icon Editions, Harper and Row, 1972.

Stolnitz, Jerome. "'Beauty': Some Stages in the History of an Idea." *Journal of the History of Ideas* 22 (1961):185–204.

Strawson, P. F. "Aesthetic Appraisal and Works of Art." In *Freedom and Resentment*. London: Methuen & Co., 1974.

Tolstoy, Leo. *What Is Art?* 1896: Reprint. New York: Bobbs-Merrill, 1960.

Tormey, Alan. "Aesthetic Rights." *Journal of Aesthetics and Art Criticism* (Winter 1973):163–170.

Urmson, J. O. "What Makes a Situation Aesthetic?" *Proceedings of the Aristotelian Society* 31 (1957):75–92.

Vendler, Helen. "The Demands of Poetry on Criticism." *Key Reporter* 43, no. 1 (Autumn 1977).

Waterhouse, Ellis. *Reynolds*. London: Phaidon, 1973.

Weitz, Morris. "The Role of Theory in Aesthetics." *Journal of Aesthetics and Art Criticism* 15, no. 1 (September 1956):27–35.

Wellek, René, and Warren, Austin. *Theory of Literature*. New York: Harcourt, Brace & Co., 1956.

Wilson, Edmund. "Marxism and Literature." *Atlantic Monthly*, December 1937. 741–750.

Wilson, Sloan. *All the Best People*. New York: Putnam, 1970.

Wimsatt, W. K. "History and Criticism." In *The Verbal Icon*. Lexington, Ky.: University of Kentucky Press, 1954.

————, and Beardsley, Monroe C. "The International Fallacy." In *The Verbal Icon*.

Wittgenstein, Ludwig. *Lectures and Conversations on Aesthetics, Psychology, and Religious Belief*. Berkeley, Calif.: University of California Press, 1972.

Wollheim, Richard, ed. *Freud: A Collection of Critical Essays*. New York: Anchor Books, Doubleday, 1974.

Ziff, Paul. "Reasons in Art Criticism." In *Philosophy and Education*, edited by Israel Scheffler. Boston: Allyn and Bacon, 1958. 219–236.

Index